B'ajlom ii Nkotz'i

GUIDE TO JEWISH
PALESTINIAN ARAMAIC

MATEO G.R. & SANDRA CHIGÜELA

1ST EDITION

XXVIII.IV.MMXXI

B'ajlom ii Nkotz'i'j Publications'

GUIDE TO JEWISH PALESTINIAN ARAMAIC

ברוך אתה יי אלהינו מלך העולם בורא פרי הגפן

-MGR-

This academic literary work is dedicated to my wife, Sandra, and our five children: Cristel, Emilio, Alejandra, Camila and Galilea. In addition, I want to dedicate this academic literary work to my nieces and my nephew: Alayah, Jamie and Christopher.

Truly you can only see the light once you have fully delved into the darkness...

ARCANUM SIT SACRAMENTUM

HABITO LA OSCURIDAD – NO ABAJO, SINO ARRIBA, ME QUEDO CON MANUSCRITOS, UN BOLÍGRAFO Y PAPELES Y CON UN MANO QUE SIEMPRE ESCRIBE, NO LE PIDO A NADIE POR NADA, NI UNA CORTEZA DE PAN, NI UN SORBO DE AGUA, PORQUE NO SOY MENDIGO...MI DIOS EL SEÑOR ME PROPORCIONA LO NECESARIO...LLEVO LLAVES A MUCHAS PUERTAS Y NO LAS ABRO, EL MISTERIO DE LOS MISTERIOS PERMANECE SIN RESOLVER...NO HE PROBADO VINO NI ME HE COMPLACIDO CON EL VICIO, EN LA OSCURIDAD ME QUEDO CON LA LUZ DE VELAS PARA GUIARME POR EL CAMINO EN CUAL ME HE EMBARCADO...TODO LO QUE HE VISTO SON LOS PECADOS DEL HOMBRE NECIO Y LOS DE LA MUJER NECIA...EN UN PAÍS EXTRANJERO A MI ALMA, PERO NO DE MI ORIGEN...SIGO EN EL CAMINO CON VELA EN MANO...EN LAS PROFUNDIDADES DE LA OSCURIDAD...AL FINAL, HE LOCALIZADO LA PUERTA ÚLTIMA...A TRAVÉS DEL UMBRAL PASARÉ...CON UNA BENDICIÓN EN MIS

LABIOS…TAL VEZ PUEDA USTÉ VERME UNA VEZ MÁS…A MENOS QUE CONTINÚE USTÉ CON UNA VIDA DE LIBERTINAJE, MALICIA Y AVARICIA…LE ESPERO EN EL OTRO LADO…TODO LO QUE DEBE USTÉ HACER ES BUSCAR EL CAMINO…EL MISMO CAMINO EN QUE ME HE EMBARCADO HACE DECADAS…SI ME ENCUENTRA USTÉ A LA DIESTRA DEL SEÑOR, NO LE NEGARÉ MI MANO NI MI ABRAZO…DESGRACIADAMENTE, DEMASIADAS SE HAN PERDIDO EN LA OSCURIDAD…TIEMPO VUELA Y NO SE PUEDE RECUPERAR…LE ESPERO EN EL MISTERIO DE MISTERIOS, MÁS ALLÁ DE LA ÚNICA PUERTA…LA PUERTA QUE ESCONDE EL LUGAR SECRETO…SEGUIRÁ SIENDO UN MISTERIO HASTA QUE LO BUSQUE USTÉ…UNO SIMPLEMENTE DEBE MIRAR DENTRO DE SÍ MISMO…¿QUIÉN SOY? ¿QUÉ SOY? ¿QUÉ SEA YO? – ESO TAMBIÉN SEGUIRÁ SIENDO UN MISTERIO MÁS ALLÁ DE LA ÚNICA PUERTA…SOLO RECUERDE USTÉ…SI BUSQUE USTÉ, ENCONTRARÁ.

M.G.R.   XVII.V.MMXX

Brief History of the Author

Mateo Russo and his wife Sandra founded 'Bajlom ii Nkotz'i'j Publications' in 2018. The organization was named using two words of Mayan origin from the Tz'utujiil Language of Guatemala. The two words tell the love story of Mateo and Sandra. 'B'ajlom' means 'Jaguar' and the word 'Nkotz'i'j' means 'My flower' which is the loving name that Mateo gave to his wife. This love story of the Jaguar and his beloved flower gave birth to the mission of Mateo to preserve indigenous languages of Guatemala and southern Mexico and to create linguistic texts that can provide a written record of specific dialects and the stories of people who are collaborators with this project. The goal is to preserve all of the indigenous languages of Guatemala and others from southern Mexico; not only through a text book or grammar book, but through poetry, songs, and many other forms of literary art and artistic expression. The goal is to give a voice to the highly marginalized indigenous people who have been highly discriminated against in all societies of Latin America. Mateo has hopes in expanding this project through time, one language at a time. Mateo's philosophy is founded in the philosophy of EZLN (The Zapatista Army of National Liberation) and through the teachings of Subcomandante Marcos the original spokesperson for EZLN. The fight of EZLN has inspired Mateo to create another front in the fight that continues: The battle to preserve and protect the remnants of our past and our perception of the world around us, our own words and those words being of our ancestors. Our indigenous linguistic history is very beautiful and it needs to be preserved, because it is our linguistic inheritance. Despite that many indigenous languages are moribund... Mateo and his wife have joined together with the fight to preserve the most important facet of the cultures of the indigenous people: Our linguistic inheritance (our mother tongues). Mateo passionately supports Indigenous Human Rights and the preservation and protection of every indigenous language of Guatemala and southern Mexico. Mateo will not rest until every indigenous language has a written literary archive and until the voice of the indigenous people is not forgotten but is permanently marked in human history.

Contact Information:

'B'ajlom ii Nkotz'i'j Publications'

biinpublications@gmail.com

biinpublications@facebook.com

If you would like to donate to our cause and give your support or if you would like to donate your time or be a literary collaborator with us, please, contact us by e-mail.

אַרְמִיָא

(Aramáyá)

Jewish Palestinian Aramaic

Textbook with a Complete
Grammar Section, a Glossary
and a Phrasebook

TABLE OF CONTENTS:

Part I

Introduction to Jewish Palestinian Aramaic

Jewish Palestinian Aramaic (ארמיא) or (Aramáyá) was a Western Aramaic Language spoken by the Jews during the Classic Era in Judea, and the Levant, specifically in Hasmonean, Herodian and Roman Judea and adjacent lands in the late first millennium BCE and later in Syria Palaestina and Palaestina Secunda in the early first millennium CE. The Son of God Text found in Qumran is written in this language as well.

There were some differences in dialect between Judea and Galilee, and most surviving texts are in the Galilean dialect. The Galilean dialect of Jewish Palestinian Aramaic was the dialect of Jesus of Nazareth.

The most notable text in the Jewish Palestinian Aramaic corpus is the Jerusalem Talmud, which is still studied in Jewish religious schools and academically, although not as widely as the Babylonian Talmud, most of which is written in Jewish Babylonian Aramaic. There are some older texts in Jewish Palestinian Aramaic, notably the Megillat Taanit: the Babylonian Talmud contains occasional quotations from these.

Many extent manuscripts in Jewish Palestinian Aramaic have been corrupted over the years of their transmission by Eastern Aramaic-speaking scribes freely correcting 'errors' they came across (these 'errors' actually being genuine Jewish Palestinian Aramaic features).

Following the Arab conquest of the country in the 7th century, Arabic gradually replaced Jewish Palestinian Aramaic and eventually all other Aramaic dialects spoken throughout the Middle East, Asia Minor and Northern Africa.

M.G.R

XXVIII.IV.MMXXI

Afro-asiatic Language Family Tree, Chart I

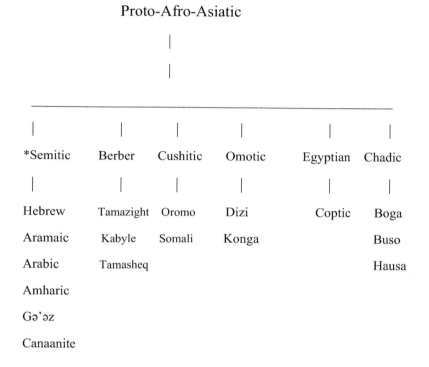

Proto-Afro-Asiatic

*Semitic	Berber	Cushitic	Omotic	Egyptian	Chadic
Hebrew	Tamazight	Oromo	Dizi	Coptic	Boga
Aramaic	Kabyle	Somali	Konga		Buso
Arabic	Tamasheq				Hausa
Amharic					
Gəʾəz					
Canaanite					

EAST SEMITIC

|

Akkadian

|

Old Akkadian

Babylonian   --

Assyrian |

WEST SEMITIC |

          | | Eblaite

     South Semitic   Central Semitic |

        /   \ /   \ |

Southwest Semitic   Arabic   Northwest Semitic

        | | |

Epigraphic   North Arabian   Amorite

South Arabian   Languages   Ugaritic

Languages   Classical Arabic   Canaanite Languages

Gə'əz | *Aramaic Languages

        | * Modern Arabic |

Modern Ethiopic   Maltese   Modern   Hebrew
Languages   Modern Aramaic

Modern South

Arabian Languages

Aramaic Languages, Chart III

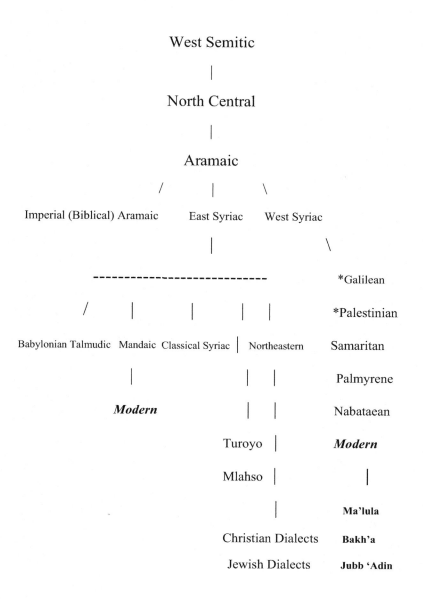

West Semitic

North Central

Aramaic

Imperial (Biblical) Aramaic   East Syriac   West Syriac

------------------------------   *Galilean

                                      *Palestinian

Babylonian Talmudic Mandaic Classical Syriac | Northeastern   Samaritan

                                                          Palmyrene

        Modern   Nabataean

                              Turoyo   *Modern*

                              Mlahso

                                                          Ma'lula

                              Christian Dialects   Bakh'a

                              Jewish Dialects   Jubb 'Adin

I)   Alphabet

Jewish Palestinian Aramaic is written in the Hebrew Alphabet which was initially developed from the Imperial Aramaic Alphabet. Hebrew had originally been written in the Paleo-Hebrew script.

History of the Modern Hebrew Alphabet

Around 500 BC, following the Achaemenid conquest of Mesopotamia under Darius I, Old Aramaic was adopted by the Persians as a "vehicle" for written communication between the different regions of the vast Persian Empire with its different peoples and languages. The use of a single official language, which modern scholarship has dubbed as Official Aramaic, Imperial Aramaic or Achaemenid Aramaic, can be assumed to have greatly contributed to the astonishing success of the Achaemenid Persians in holding their far-flung empire together for as long as they did.

Imperial Aramaic was highly standardized; its orthography was based more on historical roots than any spoken dialect and was inevitably influenced by Old Persian. The Aramaic glyph forms of the period are often divided into two main styles, the "lapidary" form, usually inscribed on hard surfaces like stone monuments, and a cursive form whose lapidary form tended to more conservative by remaining more visually similar to Phoenician and early Aramaic. Both were in use through the Achaemenid Persian period, but the cursive form steadily gained ground over the lapidary, which had largely disappeared by the 3rd century BC.

The widespread usage of Achaemenid Aramaic in the Middle East led to the gradual adoption of the Aramaic alphabet for writing Hebrew. Formerly, Hebrew had been written using an alphabet closer in form to that of Phoenician, the Paleo-Hebrew alphabet.

Today, Biblical Aramaic, Jewish Neo-Aramaic dialects and the Aramaic Language of the Talmud are written in the modern-Hebrew alphabet (distinguished from the Old Hebrew script) which is a borrowed derivative of the Imperial Aramaic Script used during the Achaemenid Persian period. The modern-Hebrew alphabet is primarily an offshoot of the original Imperial Aramaic alphabet. In classical Jewish literature, the name given to the modern-Hebrew script was "Ashurit" (the ancient Assyrian script), a script now known widely as the Aramaic script. It is believed that during the period of Assyrian dominion that the Aramaic script and language received official status. Syriac and Christian Neo-Aramaic dialects are today written in the Syriac alphabet, which has superseded the more ancient Assyrian script and now bears its name. The near-identity of the Aramaic and the classical Hebrew alphabets caused Aramaic text to be typeset mostly in the standard Hebrew script in scholarly literature.

Within this Book we will be using the modern-Hebrew alphabet for the Jewish Palestinian (Talmudic) Aramaic entries that will be displayed and analyzed throughout this text. Diacritics will not be used; however, all Aramaic vocabulary entries will be transliterated into Latin letters.

א   [alef]   (') semi-vowel

ב   [bet]   (B / V)

*this letter is spiralized and can in some cases be pronounced as 'b' and in others as 'v'

ג   [gimel]   (G)

*always pronounced as a hard 'g' like in the word 'goat'

ד   [daleth]   (D)

ה   [he]   (H)

ו   [vav]   (V / W / U / O) semi-vowel

*in Hebrew this letter can be 'v, u, o' depending on the word

ז   [zayin]   (Z)

ח   [Heth]   (Ḥ)

*pronounced like a rough throaty 'h'

ט   [Teth]   (Ṭ)

*pronounced like 't' in the word 'tough'

י   [yod]   (Y) semi-vowel

ך כ   [kaf / khaf]   (K / KH)

*this letter can be spiralized between 'c' like in the word 'cap' and a rough throaty 'h' rougher than 'ח'

ל   [lamed]   (L)

ם מ   [mem]   (M)

ן נ   [nun]   (N)

ס   [samekh]   (S)

ע   ['ayin]   (')

*this letter is a glottal stop and is pronounced like the space between the two separate sounds in the English expression 'uh-oh'

ף פ   [pe / fe]   (P / F)

*this letter can be spiralized and can be used to represent 'p' and 'f'

ץ צ   [tzadiq]   (TZ / Ṣ)

ק   [qof]   (Q)

19

ר   [resh]   (R)

שׁ   [shin / sin]   (SH / S)

*this letter can be spiralized and in some cases is pronounced like 'sh' and in some words like 's'

ת   [tav]   (T / TH)

*this letter is spiralized. In some cases, it is 't' and others 'th'

NOTES:

The block script used for Hebrew and Jewish Palestinian (Talmudic) Aramaic is, of course, not a cursive script like the alphabets of Syriac and Arabic.

1) Certain letters are Spiralized and have two separate sounds within some words. Traditionally, this sound change is indicated with a single dot that is placed in a specific place on the letter in order to indicate spiralization. The following letters are spiralized in the Modern Hebrew Alphabet.

ב   [B < V]

ך כ   [K < KH]

ף פ   [P < F]

שׁ   [SH < S]

ת   [T < TH]

2) Certain letters have two separate forms for the same letter. There is a primary form which is used at the beginning of a word and throughout the interior of a word and then the secondary form is always used at the end of a word. The following letters have a secondary form.

כ ך   [K < KH]

מ ם   [M]

נ ן   [N]

פ ף   [P < F]

צ ץ   [TZ / Ṣ]

Examples:

כל   [kol (all; every)];   לך   [lakh (for you)]

מאי   [mai? (what?)]   קם   [qam (he rose)]

נרון קיסר   [neron qeysar (Nero)]

פלח   [pəlaH (he worked)]

שתף   [shəTaf (it overflowed)]

קצץ   [qətzatz (he cut)]

22

3) The use of the 'schwa' in Semitic languages is one of the most common aspects within this linguistic family. A schwa is a neutral vowel sound that takes place within many words in Hebrew, Aramaic and Syriac. The schwa is always pronounced like the 'uh' in the English expression 'uh-oh'. Within this text the schwa will be indicated with the letter 'ə'. In the Jewish Palestinian Aramaic language, the schwa is indicated with a colon-like marking at the bottom of the letter. This same colon-like marking can also indicate that the letter is not followed by a vowel; thus, indicating a 'stop'. However, a schwa is usually pronounced when an initial consonant has the colon-like marking and the following consonant has a diacritic mark indicating an actual vowel.

Examples:

שמיא [shəmayá (heaven; sky)] schwa pronounced

איכתוב [eyktuv (I will write)] schwa not pronounced; stop indicated between 'k' and 't'

Primary vowels in Jewish Palestinian (Talmudic) Aramaic:

A – 'A' LIKE IN THE WORD 'APPLE'

Á – 'A' LONG VOWEL LIKE 'A' IN 'AWE'

E – 'E' LIKE IN THE WORD 'BED'

É – 'E' LIKE 'AI' IN THE WORD 'BAIT'; MAY INCLUDE YOD

I – 'I' LIKE 'EA' IN THE WORD 'EAT'; MAY INCLUDE YOD

O – 'O' LIKE 'OA' IN THE WORD 'BOAT'

U – 'U' LIKE 'OO' IN THE WORD 'BOOT'

AY – 'AY' LIKE 'IE' IN THE WORD 'DIE'; WILL INCLUDE YOD

*In general, these vowels are indicated via diacritic marks. In some cases, the semi-vowel consonants listed with the alphabet are used with specific words.

II)   Pronouns

Pronouns as in all languages are split up between 1st person singular and plural, 2nd person singular and plural and 3rd person singular and plural. Several pronouns in Jewish Palestinian Aramaic will differentiate between masculine and feminine.

The Pronouns (including pronominal suffixes and enclitic particles) in Jewish Palestinian Aramaic are as follows:

Example of pronouns based on number:

1st person singular = I

2nd person singular = You

3rd person singular = He / She / It

1st person plural = We

2nd person plural = You (all)

3rd person plural = They

Pronouns

1	אנא ANA	1st pers. sing.
2	את AT	2nd pers. sing. Masc. / Fem.
3	הוא היא HU' HI'	3rd pers. sing. Masc. / Fem.
1	אנן ANAN	1st pers. pl.
2	אתון אתין ATUN ATEYN	2nd pers. pl. Masc. / Fem.
3	אינון אינין INUN INEYN	3rd pers. pl. Masc. / Fem.

Copulative Pronouns

1	-נָא (Dep.) -NA	1st pers. sing.
2	-ת (Dep.) -AT	2nd pers. sing. Masc. / Fem.
3	--------------------	3rd pers. sing. Masc. / Fem.
1	-נַן (Dep.) -NAN	1st pers. pl.
2	-תוּן (Dep.) -תֵין (Dep.) -TUN -TEYN	2nd pers. pl. Masc. / Fem.
3	--------------------	3rd pers. pl. Masc. / Fem.

*Third person sing. and pl. do not have copulative pronouns or enclitic particles.

Pronominal Possessive Suffixes for Singular Nouns

1	ִי_ -i	1st pers. sing.
2	־ךְ ־יךְ -akh -ikh	2nd pers. sing. Masc. / Fem.
3	־יה ־ה -eyh -ah	3rd pers. sing. Masc. / Fem.
1	־ן -an	1st pers. pl.
2	־כון ־כין -khun -kheyn	2nd pers. pl. Masc. / Fem.
3	־הון ־הין -hun -heyn	3rd pers. pl. Masc. / Fem.

Pronominal Possessive Suffixes for Plural Nouns

1	‍ַי -ay	1st pers. sing.
2	‍ַיךְ ‍ַיכִי -aykh -aykhi	2nd pers. sing. Masc. / Fem.
3	‍ַוִי ‍ַהָא -o / -w -aha	3rd pers. sing. Masc. / Fem.
1	‍ַינָן -eynan	1st pers. pl.
2	‍ַיכוֹן ‍ַיכֵין -eykhun -eykheyn	2nd pers. pl. Masc. / Fem.
3	‍ַיהוֹן ‍ַיהֵין -eyhun -eyheyn	3rd pers. pl. Masc. / Fem.

Accusative Pronominal Suffixes

1	־נִי ־ן -ni -an	1st pers. sing.
2	־ךְ ־יךְ -akh -eykh	2nd pers. sing. Masc. / Fem.
3	־יהּ -eyh ־הּ -eh ־הּ -ah	3rd pers. sing. Masc. / Fem.
1	־נַן ־ן -nan	1st pers. pl.
2	־כוּן ־כִין -khun -akhun -khin -akhin	2nd pers. pl. Masc. / Fem.
3	־(ה)וּן ־(ה)ִין -hun / -un -hin / -in	3rd pers. pl. Masc. / Fem.

SPECIAL POSSESSOR PARTICLE

1	דִידִי DIDI	1st pers. sing.
2	דִידָך דִידִיך DIDAKH DIDIKH	2nd pers. sing. Masc. / Fem.
3	דִידִיה דִידָה DIDEYH DIDAH	3rd pers. sing. Masc. / Fem.
1	דִידָן DIDAN	1st pers. pl.
2	דִידכוֹן דִידכִין DIDKHUN DIDKHEYN	2nd pers. pl. Masc. / Fem.
3	דִידהוֹן דִידהִין DIDHUN DIDHEYN	3rd pers. pl. Masc. / Fem.

ACCUSATIVE INDEPENDENT PRONOUN

1	יתִי YATI	1st pers. sing.
2	יתָך יתִיך YATAKH YATAYKH	2nd pers. sing. Masc. / Fem.
3	יתִיה יתה YATEYH YATAH	3rd pers. sing. Masc. / Fem.
1	יתנא YATANA	1st pers. pl.
2	יתכון יתכין YATKHUN YATKHEYN	2nd pers. pl. Masc. / Fem.
3	יתהון יתהין YAT-HUN YAT-HEYN	3rd pers. pl. Masc. / Fem.

*These forms are usually used with participles similar to the Hebrew (את-) or ('ot-) form. Although these can be used; they are quite rare.

REFLEXIVE PRONOUNS

1	גרמי GARMI	Myself	1st pers. sing.
2	גרמך גרמיך GARMAKH GARMIKH	Yourself	2nd pers. sing. Masc. / Fem.
3	גרמיה גרמה GARMEYH GARMAH	Himself Herself	3rd pers. sing. Masc. / Fem.
1	גרמן GARMAN	Ourselves	1st pers. pl.
2	גרמיכון גרמיכין GARMEYKHUN GARMEYKHEYN	Yourselves	2nd pers. pl. Masc. / Fem.
3	גרמיהון גרמיהין GARMEYHUN GARMEYHEYN	Themselves	3rd pers. pl. Masc. / Fem.

INSEPARABLE PARTICLES:

Aramaic has five 'inseparable particles':

בְּ-   [B-] in, with

לְ-   [L-] to, for

דְ-   [D-] of

וְ-   [V- / W-] and

כְּ-   [K-] as

These particles will usually be followed by a 'schwa' or neutral vowel.

דְמַלְכָּא

[**Də**-Malká] = of the King

When the first consonant of word lacks a vowel, then an 'a' will follow the 'inseparable particle'

בְּמְדִינְתָּא

[**B**amdintá] = in the city

Two 'inseparable particles' can precede the same word.
Previous rules still apply.

ודמלכא

[**Wad**malká] = and of the King

ובמדינתא

[**Wə**bamdintá] = and in the city

When the initial letter in a word is an 'alef' the vowel will
carry over to the 'inseparable particle.'

דאלהא

[**D**-eláhá] = of God

When the initial letter of the word is a 'yod' then the vowel
will carry over to the 'inseparable particle.'

ד- + ידע

[D- + Yədaᵓ]

דידע

[Didaᵓ] = who knew

III)   Prepositions

The following list of prepositions are the most commonly used prepositions in Aramaic. Several are merely a single consonant that is connected to a noun. A 'schwa' or neutral vowel sound is usually the sound that follows after these types of prepositions, but there may also be a vowel shift or a word that begins with a vowel may be blended (See 'inseparable particles' in previous chapter).

Inseparable Particles are always attached to a noun. Many other prepositions do not attach to a noun and they can stand alone.

Most prepositions can connect with pronominal suffixes. Here is a small chart of pronominal suffixes that are used in Aramaic:

There are two types of Pronominal Suffixes:

Singular Possessive Suffixes for Prepositions

1	־ִי -i	1st pers. sing.
2	־ָךְ ־ִיךְ -akh -ikh	2nd pers. sing. Masc. / Fem.
3	־ֵיה ־ָה -eyh -ah	3rd pers. sing. Masc. / Fem.
1	־ָן -an	1st pers. pl.
2	־כוּן ־כִין -khun -kheyn	2nd pers. pl. Masc. / Fem.
3	־הוּן ־הִין -hun -heyn	3rd pers. pl. Masc. / Fem.

Plural Possessive Suffixes for Prepositions

1	יַ־ -ay	1st pers. sing.
2	־יךְ ־יכִי -aykh -aykhi	2nd pers. sing. Masc. / Fem.
3	־יו ־הָא -o / -w -aha	3rd pers. sing. Masc. / Fem.
1	־ינַן -eynan	1st pers. pl.
2	־יכוֹן ־יכִין -eykhun -eykheyn	2nd pers. pl. Masc. / Fem.
3	־יהוֹן ־יהִין -eyhun -eyheyn	3rd pers. pl. Masc. / Fem.

-בְּ   (B-)   [in, with]

*This form may have all **singular** pronominal suffixes attached.

-לְ   (L-)   [to, for]

*This form may have all **singular** pronominal suffixes attached.

מִן   (Min) [from]

*This form may have all **singular** pronominal suffixes attached.

מֶנִּי   [from me] = Meni

עִם   [with; along with]

*This form may have all **singular** pronominal suffixes attached.

עִמִּי   [with me] = 'Imi

בִּגְלַל   [for the sake of; because of] = Biglal

*This form may accept all **singular** suffixes

בֵּין   [among, between] = Beyn

*Takes all **singular** suffixes

בֵּינִי   [among, between] = Beyney

*This form takes all **plural** suffixes

-כְ   [as] = K-

*this form is only used with nouns

כְּוֹת-   [as; like] = Kəvat- (Kəwat-)

*This form can be used with all **singular** suffixes

עַל [upon, concerning, over, unto] = 'Al

*This form is not used with suffixes

עָלַי- [upon, concerning, over, unto] = 'Alay-

*This form is attached to all **plural** suffixes; the 1st person singular is pronounced ['Alay]

תַּחְתּוֹתִי [under] = TəHotey

*This form does not take suffixes

תַּחְוֹת- [under] = TəHoth-

*This form accepts all **plural** suffixes

קֶדֶם [before] = Qadam; Qadm-

*This form accepts all **plural** suffixes

בתר [after] = Bátar, Bátra-

*This form accepts all **singular** suffixes

1	בתרי	בתרן
2m	בתרך	בתרכון
2f	בתריך	בתרכין
3m	בתריה	בתרהון
3f	בתרה	בתרהין

1	Bátri	Bátran
2m	Bátrakh	Bátarkhon
2f	Bátrikh	Bátarkheyn
3m	Bátreyh	Bátarhun
3f	Bátrah	Bátarheyn

קְבֵל [against] = Qabel, Qabl-

Qabl- receives **singular** pronominal suffixes.

חֲלָף [instead of; on behalf of] = Halaf, Half-

*This preposition takes **plural** pronominal suffixes

כְּגוֹן [like] = Kəgon

*This preposition is independent and will not receive suffixes

כְּמִין [like; as] = Kəmin

*This preposition is independent and will not receive suffixes

Other constructions:

כְּל-   [all (of)] = Kol

*This form can be used with all **singular** pronominal suffixes

*This preposition can be used by itself without a suffix and it can carry the meaning of 'all' [used with emphatic state nouns] and 'every' [used with absolute state nouns]

כל כתב

[Kol Kətav] = Every Book [absolute state]

כליה כתבא

[Koleyh Kətava] = the Whole Book

כלהון כתביא

[Koləhun Kətáváyá] = All of the Books

אית [There is / are] = It

*This verb can have a special construction that carries the meaning of 'to exist' and it can stand alone and use the preposition (-ל) or (L-) with a suffix in order to carry the meaning 'to have'

'TO EXIST' (IS, AM, ARE)

1	איתנא ITNA	1st pers. sing.
2	אית את IT AT	2nd pers. sing. Masc. / Fem.
3	איתיה איתה ITEYH ITAH	3rd pers. sing. Masc. / Fem.
1	איתנן ITNAN	1st pers. pl.
2	איתנכון איתנכין ITANKHUN ITANKHIN	2nd pers. pl. Masc. / Fem.
3	איתנהון איתנהין ITANHUN ITANHIN	3rd pers. pl. Masc. / Fem.

*Usually, the verb stands alone and does not receive a suffix and the pronoun is attached to (‎לְ‑). Thus, giving the meaning 'there is to me' – (אִית לִי) 'I have'

מלכא איתיה

[Malka iteyh] = He is the King

איתיה גוברא

[Iteyh guvrá] = He is a man

איתה אמי

[Itah imi] = She is my mother

איתנן גובריא

[Itnan guvráyá] = We are men

...אית לי

[It li…] = I have…

...אית לך

[It lakh…] = You have…

...אית לן

[It lan…] = We have

RANDOM CONSTRUCTIONS BASED ON THE JERUSALEM TALMUD:

לא + אית = לית

[Leyt = It + La] = There is / are not...

אין

[Eyn] = Not; Nothing

איניה

[Eyneyh] = He is not

את = אנת

[At = Ant] = You

'אנת' (Ant) is an alternate version of 'את' (At) and is very similar to the pronoun used in Classical Syriac. However, true to the spelling, Syriac tends to not pronounce the 'nun'.

אִין   [In] = Yes

+ אִין   [In + (enclitic)]

אִיננָא   [In-ná] = Yes, I am

אִיננַן   [In-nan] = Yes, we are

לִי = לִית

[Leyt = Ley] = There is / are not…

1st pers. sing. & pl.	לֵינָא LEYNA = I AM NOT	לֵינָן LEYNAN = WE ARE NOT
2nd pers. sing. & pl.	לֵית אַת לֵית אַנְת LEYT AT = YOU ARE NOT LEYT ANT (alt.)	לֵיתַנְכוֹן לֵיתַנְכִין LEYTANKHUN = YOU ARE NOT LEYTANKHIN = YOU ARE NOT
3rd pers. sing & pl.	לֵיתֵיהּ לֵיתַהּ LEYTEYH = HE IS NOT LEYTAH = SHE IS NOT	לֵיתַנְהוֹן לֵיתַנְהִין LEYTANHUN = THEY ARE NOT LEYTANHIN = THEY ARE NOT

IV) Nouns

All Nouns in Aramaic are either masculine or feminine. All Nouns in Aramaic are inflected according to gender, number and state. Gender [Masculine or Feminine], Number [Singular or Plural] and State [Absolute, Emphatic or Construct].

Nouns in Aramaic have three states: absolute, emphatic and construct. Absolute is the basic core root of the noun and it is used in specific situations. Emphatic is the basic form of all nouns in Aramaic and it is the form that is used in most dictionaries. Construct is a special form that is used somewhat like the Genitive Case in most case languages.

כתבא

[Kətává]

Book [m.]

מלכתא

[Malkthá]

Queen [f.]

	Sing.	Pl.
Absolute	כתב	כתבין
Emphatic	כתבא	כתביא
Construct	כתב	כתבי

	Sing.	Pl.
Absolute	מלכה	מלכן
Emphatic	מלכתא	מלכתא
Construct	מלכת	מלכת

Transliteration:

	Sing.	Pl.
Absolute	KƎTAV	KƎTAVIN
Emphatic	KƎTAVA	KƎTAVAYA
Construct	KƎTAV	KƎTAVEY

	Sing.	Pl.
Absolute	MALKAH	MALKAN
Emphatic	MALKTHA	MALKATHA
Construct	MALKATH	MALKHATH

טליא   טליתא

[Talyá]   [Talitha]

Boy [m.]   Girl [f.]

	Sing.	Pl.
Absolute	טלי	טלין
Emphatic	טליא	טליא
Construct	טלי	טליי

	Sing.	Pl.
Absolute	טליה	טלין
Emphatic	טליתא	טליתא
Construct	טלית	טלית

Transliteration:

	Sing.	Pl.
Absolute	ṬƏLEY	ṬƏLIN
Emphatic	ṬALYÁ	ṬALÁYÁ
Construct	ṬƏLEY	ṬALYEY

	Sing.	Pl.
Absolute	ṬALYAH	ṬALYAN
Emphatic	ṬALITHÁ	ṬALYÁTHÁ
Construct	ṬALYATH	ṬALYÁTH

רעיא

[Ra'ayá]

Shepherd [m.]

מלכותא

[Malkuthá]

Kingdom [f.]

	Sing.	Pl.
Absolute	רעי	רעיין
Emphatic	רעיא	רעיתא
Construct	רעי	רעוי

	Sing.	Pl.
Absolute	מלכו	מלכוון
Emphatic	מלכותא	מלכוותא
Construct	מלכות	מלכוות

Transliteration:

	Sing.	Pl.
Absolute	RA'EY	RA'AYÁYN
Emphatic	RA'AYÁ	RA'AYÁTHÁ
Construct	RA'EY	RA'AWEY

	Sing.	Pl.
Absolute	MALKU	MALKWAN
Emphatic	MALKUTHÁ	MALKWATHÁ
Construct	MALKUTH	MALKWATH

מצראה   מצריתא

[Mitzra'ah]   [Mitzreythá]

Egyptian man [m.]   Egyptian woman [f.]

	Sing.	Pl.
Absolute	מצרי	מצראיין
Emphatic	מצראה	מצריא

	Sing.	Pl.
Absolute	מצריה	מצרין
Emphatic	מצריתא	מצריתא

Transliteration:

	Sing.	Pl.
Absolute	MITZRAY	MITZRAYIN
Emphatic	MITZRÁ'ÁH	MITZRÁYÁ

	Sing.	Pl.
Absolute	MITZRAYAH	MITZRAYÁN
Emphatic	MITZREYTHÁ	MITZREYÁTHÁ

Although the majority of nouns in Aramaic follow the previous guidelines, there are always exceptions:

Some nouns have irregular forms such as the following words:

אבא   [Aba] = Father

אבהתא   [Abahatha] = Fathers

אמא   [Ima] = Mother

אמהתא   [Imahatha] = Mothers

ברא   [Bəra] = Son

בנייא   [Bənayya] = Sons

ברתא   [Bəratha] = Daughter

בנתא   [Bənatha] = Daughters

איתתא   [Int-tha] = Wife

נשיא   [Nəshaya] = Wives

Some feminine nouns may only look masculine in their plural form and not in their singular form:

מִילְתָא   [Melthá] = word [feminine]

מִילַיָא   [Meláyá] = words [feminine, but looks like masculine plural]

GENITIVE RELATION IN CLASSICAL ARAMAIC:

THREE WAYS: 1) Construct, 2) With (-ד) and emphatic

& 3) With (-ד) and emphatic with pronominal suffix

The King's Book =

כתב מלכא   [Kətáv Malká] Construct (1)

כתבא דמלכא   [Kətává dəmalká] (2)

כתביה דמלכא   [Kətáveyh dəmalká] (3)

The King of Kings

מלך מלכיא   [Melekh Malkáyá] Construct (1)

מלכא דמלכיא   [Malká dəmalkáyá] (2)

מלכהון דמלכא   [Malk-hun dəmalkáyá] (3)

CONSTRUCT FORM:

The construct form is a shortened form of the noun. Some vowels in the emphatic form will move over to the next consonant and some are irregular.

Ex.

אבא   [Abá] = Father

אב   [Ab] = Father (Construct)

אבהת   [Abahath] = Fathers (Construct)

אמא   [Imá] = Mother

אם   [Em] = Mother (Construct)

אמהת   [Imahath] = Mothers (Construct)

שמא   [Shəmá] = Name

שם   [Shem] = Name (Construct)

שמי   [Shəmey] = Names (Construct)

ברא   [Bərá] = Son

בר   [Bar] = Son (Construct)

בני   [Bəney] = Sons (Construct)

*Remember that these forms are used to create a form of the Genitive

שם אלהא

[Shem Eláhá] = Name of God

בית לחם

[Beyth LeHem] = Bethlehem (House of Bread)

אם ישוע

[Em Yəshuᵓ] = Mother of Jesus

V) Nouns with Pronominal Suffixes

The following section will demonstrate how Pronominal Suffixes are used with nouns:

Charts for the Pronominal Suffixes:

Pronominal Possessive Suffixes for Singular Nouns

1	‫ִי‬- -i	1st pers. sing.
2	‫ְ‬‫ך‬- ‫ִ‬‫יך‬- -akh -ikh	2nd pers. sing. Masc. / Fem.
3	‫ָיה‬- ‫ָ‬‫ה‬- -eyh -ah	3rd pers. sing. Masc. / Fem.
1	‫ָ‬‫ן‬- -an	1st pers. pl.
2	‫ְכון‬- ‫ְכין‬- -khun -kheyn	2nd pers. pl. Masc. / Fem.
3	‫ְהון‬- ‫ְהין‬- -hun -heyn	3rd pers. pl. Masc. / Fem.

Pronominal Possessive Suffixes for Plural Nouns

1	יַ־ -ay	1st pers. sing.
2	־יך ־יכִי -aykh -aykhi	2nd pers. sing. Masc. / Fem.
3	־יו ־הָא -o / -w -aha	3rd pers. sing. Masc. / Fem.
1	־ינָן -eynan	1st pers. pl.
2	־יכון ־יכִין -eykhun -eykheyn	2nd pers. pl. Masc. / Fem.
3	־יהון ־יהִין -eyhun -eyheyn	3rd pers. pl. Masc. / Fem.

With the noun: כתבא [Kətává] = Book (sing.)

כתביא [Kətáváyá] = Books (plural)

	Sing. Pronoun	Pl. Pronoun
1	כתבי	כתבן
2m	כתבך	כתבכון
2f	כתביך	כתבכין
3m	כתביה	כתבהון
3f	כתבה	כתבהין

Pl. Noun

	Sing. Pronoun	Pl. Pronoun
1	כתבי	כתבינן
2m	כתביך	כתביכון
2f	כתביכי	כתביכין
3m	כתבוי	כתביהון
3f	כתבהא	כתביהין

Transliteration:

	Sing. Pronoun	Pl. Pronoun
1	KƏTAVI	KƏTÁVAN
2m	KƏTÁVÁKH	KƏTÁVKHUN
2f	KƏTÁVIKH	KƏTÁVKHEYN
3m	KƏTÁVEYH	KƏTÁVHUN
3f	KƏTÁVÁH	KƏTÁVHEYN

Pl. Noun

1	KƏTÁVAY	KƏTÁVEYNAN
2m	KƏTÁVAYKH	KƏTÁVEYKHUN
2f	KƏTÁVAYKHI	KƏTÁVEYKHEYN
3m	KƏTÁVO	KƏTÁVEYHUN
3f	KƏTÁVÁHÁ	KƏTÁVEYHEYN

With the noun: מלכתא [Malkthá] = Queen (sing.)

מלכתא [Malkáthá] = Queens (plural)

	Sing. Pronoun	Pl. Pronoun
1	מלכתי	מלכתן
2m	מלכתך	מלכתכון
2f	מלכתיך	מלכתכין
3m	מלכתיה	מלכתהון
3f	מלכתה	מלכתהין

Pl. Noun

1	מלכתי	מלכתן
2m	מלכתך	מלכתכון
2f	מלכתיך	מלכתכין
3m	מלכתיה	מלכתהון
3f	מלכתה	מלכתהין

Transliteration:

	Sing. Pronoun	Pl. Pronoun
1	MALKTI	MALKTAN
2m	MALKTAKH	MALKATKHUN
2f	MALKTIKH	MALKATKHEYN
3m	MALKTEYH	MALKAT-HUN
3f	MALKTAH	MALKAT-HEYN

Pl. Noun

1	MALKHATI	MALKHÁTÁN
2m	MALKHÁTAKH	MALKHÁTKHUN
2f	MALKHÁTIKH	MALKHÁTKHEYN
3m	MALKHÁTEYH	MALKHÁT-HUN
3f	MALKHÁTAH	MALKHÁT-HEYN

Some nouns have an irregular form when a possessive suffix is attached:

אבא   [Abá] = Father [m.]

אבי   [Abi] = My Father

אבוך   [Abukh] = Your Father [m.]

אבוכי   [Abukhi] = Your Father [f.]

אביה   [Abeyh] = His Father [m.]

אבוה   [Abuh] = Her Father [f.]

אבונן   [Abunan] = Our Father

אבוכון   [Abukhun] = Your Father [m.pl.]

אבוכין   [Abukheyn] = Your Father [f.pl.]

אבוהון   [Abuhun] = Their Father [m.pl.]

אבוהין   [Abuheyn] = Their Father [f.pl.]

אָחָא [AHá] = Brother [m.]

This noun is inflected in the same manner as (אַבָּא) 'Father'

אָחִי [AHi] = My Brother

אָחוּךְ [AHukh] = Your Brother [m.]

אָחוּכִי [AHukhi] = Your Brother [f.]

אָחֵיהּ [AHeyh] = His Brother [m.]

אָחוּי [AHo] = His Brothers [m.] Plural Noun

VI)   Adjectives

Adjectives always come after the noun and will match the noun in gender and number. Adjectives, as well, have three states that correspond with the states of nouns.

The following will be a chart of the three different states that an adjective can be in; including gender and number.

טב [Tav] *Good* (adj.)

MASCULINE

	Sing.	Pl.
Absolute	טב	טבין
Emphatic	טבא	טביא
Construct	טב	טבי

FEMININE

	Sing.	Pl.
Absolute	טבא	טבן
Emphatic	טבתא	טבתא
Construct	טבת	טבת

Transliteration of previous page:

MASCULINE

	Sing.	Pl.
Absolute	TÁV	TÁVIN
Emphatic	TÁVÁ	TÁVÁYÁ
Construct	TÁV	TÁVEY

FEMININE

	Sing.	Pl.
Absolute	TÁVÁ	TÁVÁN
Emphatic	TÁVTHÁ	TÁVÁTHÁ
Construct	TÁVATH	TÁVÁTH

NOTE: REMEMBER THAT SOME FEMININE NOUNS
MAY LOOK AND MAY BE INFLECTED LIKE
MASCULINE NOUNS. DESPITE APPEARING TO BE A
MASCULINE NOUN, THEY WILL STILL USE
FEMININE ADJECTIVES. ALL OF THESE TYPES OF
NOUNS WILL BE PROPERLY MARKED AS FEMININE
IN THE GLOSSARY.

Some Adjectives will end in a 'yod' in the Glossary Section.
The Masculine and Feminine forms of such verbs will be as
follows:

אַרְמִי   [Arami] *Aramean* (adj.)

אַרְמָיָא   [Aramáyá] *Aramean –* **masculine emphatic**

אַרְמִיתָא   [Arameythá] *Aramean –* **feminine emphatic**

ADJECTIVES BEING USED AS NOUNS:

ADJECTIVES CAN ALSO BE USED AS NOUNS –

ביש   [BISH] EVIL (ADJ.)

בישא   [BISHÁ] THE EVIL ONE [NOUN]

טב   [TÁV] GOOD (ADJ.)

טבא   [TÁVÁ] THE GOOD ONE [NOUN]

שפיר   [SHAFIR] BEAUTIFUL (ADJ.)

שפירא   [SHAFIRÁ] THE BEAUTIFUL ONE [NOUN]

קדוש   [QƏDOSH] HOLY (ADJ.)

קדושא   [QƏDOSHÁ] THE HOLY ONE (ADJ.)

רב   [RAB] GREAT (ADJ.)

רבא   [RABÁ] THE GREAT ONE, MASTER [NOUN]

VII) This and That, Here and There

The following will be the basic words used to express 'this' and 'that', and 'here' and 'there.'

THIS AND THAT, THESE AND THOSE

MASC. THIS	דְנָא = DƏNA דֵין = DEYN	הָדֵין = HADEYN הָהָן = HAHAN
FEM. THIS	דָא = DA	הָדָא = HADA
PL. THESE	אִילֵין = ILEYN	הָלֵין = HALEYN

MASC. THAT	הָהוּא = HAHU	הָךְ = HAKH אִידָךְ = IDEYKH הָדָךְ = HADEYKH יָתֵיה = YATEYH
FEM. THAT	הָהִיא = HAHI	הָךְ = HAKH יָתַה = YATAH
PL. THOSE	הִינוּן = HINEYN אִינוּן = INEYN	

*The initial letters 'א' and 'ה' disappear after the prepositions: (ב | ד | ו | לְ)

*(אִידָךְ | הָךְ | דְנָא | דֵין) are only used substantively and all the others are used adjectivally and substantively.

HERE AND THERE

כָּא

[Ka] = Here

לְכָא

[Ləkha] = Hither

הָכָא

[Hakha] = Here

לְהָכָא

[Ləhakha] = Hither

תַּמָן

[Thaman] = There

לְתַמָן

[Ləthaman] = Thither

הַלָן

[Halán] = There

לְהַלָן

[Ləhalán] = Thither

Examples:

תָּא לְהָכָא!   [Tha ləhakha!] = Come here!

זִיל לְתַמָן!   [Zel ləthamán!] = Go there!

VIII) Interrogatives

The following is a list of Interrogatives that are used in Jewish Palestinian Aramaic.

הֵיכָן?

[Heykhan?] = Where?

הַיְדָא?

[Hayda?] = Where?

הַיְדֵי?

[Haydey?] = Where?

אָן?

[An?] = Where?

הֵן?

[Han?] = Where?

הֵיכָא?

[Heykhah?] = Where?

ל- + אָן?　　　　[Lə- + An]

לְאָן?

[Lə'an?] = To where? Whither?

מְנָא

[Mina?] = Whence? From where?

מִנָּן?

[Minan?] = Whence? From where?

מְנָן?

[Mənan?] = Whence? From where?

80

מן היכא?

[Min Heykha?] = From where?

מה?

[Mah?] = What?

מאי?

[Mai?] = What?

מא?

[Ma?] = What?

מנא?

[Maná?] = What?

מן?

[Man?] = What?

מַהוּ?

[Mahu?] = What is it?

לָמָה?

[Ləmah?] = Why? For what?

לְמַנָא?

[Ləmaná?] = Why?

מַאן?

[Man?] = Who?

מַהַן?

[Mahan?] = Who?

מַן?

[Man?] = Who?

מַנּוּ?

[Mano?] = Who is it? Who is he?

אֵימַת?

[Eymat?] = When?

הַיְידֵין?

[Haydeyn?] = Which? [masculine]

הַיְידָא?

[Hayda?] = Which? [feminine]

אַיְילֵין?

[Ayleyn?] = Which? [plural]

אֵיךְ?

[Eykh?] = How?

הֵיךְ?

[Heykh?] = How?

אֵיכֵי?

[Eykhey?] = How?

הֵיכֵי?

[Heykhey?] = How?

הֵיכֵין?

[Heykheyn?] = How?

עִם מָאן?

['Im man?] = With whom?

מִן מָאן?

[Min man?] = From whom?

דמאן?

[Dəman?] = Whose?

כמה?

[Kəmah?] = How many? How much?

IX)   Sentence Structure

Although Aramaic Sentence Structure is quite flexible, the most common word order would have the verb begin the sentence very much like Arabic and Biblical Hebrew.

V-S-O [VERB-SUBJECT-OBJECT]

וחמא אלהא כל כל מא דאת עבדתה

[wa-**Həmá** *eláhá* <u>kol ma</u> də-At ʻabadthah]

[and-**(he)** **saw**-*God*-<u>everything</u> that you did]

> **V** - *S* - <u>O</u>

*This tends to be the word order as long as there is a Direct Object in the Sentence and a Verb

Due to the flexibility of Aramaic, the word order can also be:

S-V-O [SUBJECT-VERB-OBJECT]

ואלהא חמא כל מא דאת עבדתה

[wa-*eláhá* **Həmá** <u>kol ma</u> də-At ʻabadthah]

[and-*God*-**(he)** **saw**-<u>everything</u> that you did]

> *S* - **V** - <u>O</u>

Without a Verb in the Sentence and with statements such as

'the king is good' there are two ways that this statement can be written.

טב מלכא   [Adj. + Noun]

[Tav Malka] = the King is good [traditional]

מלכא טב   [Noun + Adj.]

[Malka Tav] = the King is good [alternate]

*In order to create a statement such as this the noun stays in the emphatic state and the adjective will be changed to the absolute state.

מלכא [King (n) emphatic / normal state]

טבא   [good (adj.) emphatic / normal state]

טב [good (adj.) absolute]

With sentences that lack a Verb, but have a preposition:

SUBJECT – PREPOSITION-?

EX.

אנא מן ירושלם

[Ana min Yərushlem] = I am from Jerusalem

X) Verbs: Perfect, Imperfect & Participles

All verbs in Aramaic follow a selection of patterns.

I.	PE'AL	Simple
II.	ETHPE'EL	Simple Passive
III.	PA'EL	Intensive
IV.	ETHPA'AL	Intensive Passive
V.	APH'EL	Causative
VI.	ETTAPH'AL	Causative Passive

*Perfect (Past Tense), Imperfect (Future Tense), Participles (Present Tense)

*The Verb (פעל), which means 'to labor' is used by linguists in order to differentiate the patterns visually.

*These names are spelled conventionally. More correctly they would be:

P°al, Ethp°el, Pa°°el, Ethpa°°al, Ap°el & Ettap°al

There are also several kinds of verbs called 'Weak Verbs' that will follow certain patterns based on certain irregularities. These types of verbs are:

1.	PE-NUN	נפק	[nəfaq]
2.	PE-ALAPH	אכל	[akhal]
3.	PE-YOD	יתב	[yətav]
4.	'E-ALAPH	שאל	[sha'l]
5.	HOLLOW ['E-WAW]	קם (קום)	[qam (qum)]
6.	GEMINATE	עלל	['alal]
7.	LAMAD-YOD	צלי / אתא	[ata / tzalley]

PERFECT TENSE SUFFIXES

1	‎-ית‎ -ETH	**1st pers. sing.**
2	‎-תה‎ ‎-ת‎ -TAH -T	**2nd pers. sing.** **Masc. / Fem.**
3	‎-‎ ‎-ת‎ - -AT	**3rd pers. sing.** **Masc. / Fem.**
1	‎-נן‎ -NAN	**1st pers. pl.**
2	‎-תון‎ ‎-תין‎ -TUN -TEYN	**2nd pers. pl.** **Masc. / Fem.**
3	‎-ון‎ ‎-ן‎ -UN -AN	**3rd pers. pl.** **Masc. / Fem.**

IMPERFECT TENSE PREFIXES

1	אִי- E-	1st pers. sing.
2	תְ- תְ- יִן T- T- ...IN	2nd pers. sing. Masc. / Fem.
3	יְ- תְ- Y- T-	3rd pers. sing. Masc. / Fem.
1	נְ- N-	1st pers. pl.
2	תְ- וּן תְ- ן T- ...UN T- ...AN	2nd pers. pl. Masc. / Fem.
3	יְ- וּן יְ- ן Y- ...UN Y- ...AN	3rd pers. pl. Masc. / Fem.

PERFECT TENSE

1	פעלית PE'LETH	1ˢᵗ pers. sing.	I labored
2	פעלתה פעלת PA'ALTAH PA'ALT	2ⁿᵈ pers. sing. Masc. / Fem.	You labored
3	פעל פעלת PA'AL PA'LAT	3ʳᵈ pers. sing. Masc. / Fem.	He / She labored
1	פעלנן PA'ALNAN	1ˢᵗ pers. pl.	We labored
2	פעלתון פעלתין PA'ALTUN PA'ALTEYN	2ⁿᵈ pers. pl. Masc. / Fem.	You all labored
3	פעלון פעלן PA'ƏLUN PA'ƏLAN	3ʳᵈ pers. pl. Masc. / Fem.	They labored

IMPERFECT TENSE

1	איפעל EF'AL	1st pers. sing.	I will labor
2	תפעל תפעלין TIF'AL TIF'ƏLIN	2nd pers. sing. Masc. / Fem.	You will labor
3	יפעל תפעל YIF'AL TIF'AL	3rd pers. sing. Masc. / Fem.	He / She will labor
1	נפעל NIF'AL	1st pers. pl.	We will labor
2	תפעלון תפעלן TIF'ƏLUN TIF'ƏLAN	2nd pers. pl. Masc. / Fem.	You all will labor
3	יפעלון יפעלן YIF'ƏLUN YIF'ƏLAN	3rd pers. pl. Masc. / Fem.	They will labor

PARTICIPLES

Masc.	פָּעִיל PA'EL	'laboring' 'laborer'
Fem.	פָּעְלָה PA'ƏLAH	'laboring' 'laborer'
Masc. Pl.	פָּעְלִין PA'ƏLIN	'laboring' 'laborers'
Fem. Pl.	פָּעְלָן PA'ƏLAN	'laboring' 'laborers'

IMPERATIVES

Masc.	פְּעַל PƏ'AL	Labor! Work!
Fem.	פָּעְלִין PA'ƏLIN	Labor! Work!
Pl.	פָּעְלוּן PA'ƏLUN	Labor! Work!

PERFECT TENSE VERB 'TO WRITE'

1	כתבית KETBEYTH	1st pers. sing.	I wrote
2	כתבתה כתבת KATAVTAH KATAVT	2nd pers. sing. Masc. / Fem.	You wrote
3	כתב בתבת KATAV KATVAT	3rd pers. sing. Masc. / Fem.	He / She wrote
1	כתבנן KATAVNAN	1st pers. pl.	We wrote
2	כתבתון כתבתין KATAVTUN KATAVTEYN	2nd pers. pl. Masc. / Fem.	You all wrote
3	כתבון בתבן KATƏVUN KATƏVAN	3rd pers. pl. Masc. / Fem.	They wrote

IMPERFECT TENSE VERB 'TO WRITE'

1	איכתוב EYKTUV	1ˢᵗ pers. sing.	I will write
2	תכתוב תכתבין TIKTUV TIKTƏVIN	2ⁿᵈ pers. sing. Masc. / Fem.	You will write
3	יכתוב תכתוב YIKTUV TIKTUV	3ʳᵈ pers. sing. Masc. / Fem.	He / She will write
1	נכתוב NIKTUV	1ˢᵗ pers. pl.	We will write
2	תכתבון תכתבן TIKTƏVUN TIKTƏVAN	2ⁿᵈ pers. pl. Masc. / Fem.	You all will write
3	יכתבון יכתבן YIKTƏVUN YIKTƏVAN	3ʳᵈ pers. pl. Masc. / Fem.	They will write

PARTICIPLE OF VERB 'TO WRITE'

Masc.	כתיב KATEYV	'writing' 'writer'
Fem.	כתבה KATVAH	'writing' 'writer'
Masc. Pl.	כתבין KATVIN	'writing' 'writers'
Fem. Pl.	כתבן KATVAN	'writing' 'writers'

IMPERATIVE OF VERB 'TO WRITE'

Masc.	כתוב KƏTUV	Write!
Fem.	כותבין KUTVIN	Write!
Pl.	כותבון KUTVUN	Write!

*The following section will be verb conjugation based upon each individual verbal pattern

PE'AL VERBS (כתב) to Write

Perfect

	Sing.	Plural
1	כתבית	כתבנן
2m	כתבתה	כתבתון
2f	כתבת	כתבתין
3m	כתב	כתבון
3f	כתבת	כתבן

Imperfect

	Sing.	Plural
1	איכתוב	נכתוב
2m	תכתוב	תכתבון
2f	תכתבין	תכתבן
3m	יכתוב	יכתבון
3f	תכתוב	יכתבן

Participles

	Sing.	Plural
Masc.	כתיב	כתבין
Fem.	כתבה	כתבן

Imperative

Masc.	כתוב
Fem.	כותבין
Plural	בותבון

Infinitive	למכתב

Transliteration:

Perfect

	Sing.	Plural
1	ketbeth	katavnan
2m	katavthah	katavthun
2f	katavth	katavtheyn
3m	katav	katavun
3f	katvat	katavan

Imperfect

	Sing.	Plural
1	eyktuv	niktuv
2m	tiktuv	tiktvun
2f	tiktvin	tiktvan
3m	yiktuv	yiktvun
3f	tiktuv	yiktvan

Participles

	Sing.	Plural
Masc.	katev	katvin
Fem.	katvah	katvan

Imperative

Masc.	ktuv
Fem.	kutvin
Plural	kutvun

Infinitive   ləmaktav

NOTE: MANY PE'AL VERBS WILL MAINTAIN A
DIFFERENT ROOT VOWEL IN THE IMPERFECT TENSE.
THE EXAMPLES SHOWN UP ABOVE ARE OF AN 'O'
ROOT VERB. ALL VERBS LIKE THIS WILL BE MARKED
IN THE GLOSSARY WITH THEIR APPROPRIATE ROOT
VOWEL.

A-ROOT   (a)

U/O-ROOT   (u/o)

E-ROOT   (e)

ETHPE'EL VERBS (איתכתב) to Be Written

Perfect

	Sing.	Plural
1	איתכתבית	איתכתבנן
2m	איתכתבת	איתכתבתון
2f	איתכתבת	איתכתבתין
3m	איתכתיב	איתכתבון
3f	איתכתיבת	איתכתבן

Imperfect

	Sing.	Plural
1	אתכתיב	נתכתיב
2m	תתכתיב	תתכתבון
2f	תתכתבין	תתכתבן
3m	יתכתיב	יתכתבון
3f	תתכתיב	יתכתבן

Participles

	Sing.	Plural
Masc.	מתכתיב	מתכתבין
Fem.	מתכתיבה	מתכתבן

Imperative

Masc.	איתכתיב
Fem.	איתכתבין
Plural	איתכתבון

| Infinitive | למתכתבה |

Transliteration

Perfect

	Sing.	Plural
1	ithkatveth	ithktevnan
2m	ithktevth	ithktevthun
2f	ithktevth	ithktevtheyn
3m	ithktev	ithktevun
3f	ithkatvath	ithktevan

Imperfect

	Sing.	Plural
1	ithktev	nithktev
2m	tithktev	tithktevun
2f	tithkatvin	tithktevan
3m	yithktev	yithktevun
3f	tithktev	yithktevan

Participles

	Sing.	Plural
Masc.	mithktev	mithkatvin
Fem.	mithkatvah	mithkatván

Imperative

Masc.	ithktev
Fem.	ithkatvin
Plural	ithkatvun

Infinitive	ləmithktavah

PA'EL VERBS (בריך) to Bless

Perfect

	Sing.	Plural
1	ברכית	ברכנן
2m	ברכתה	ברכתון
2f	ברכת	ברכתין
3m	בריך	ברכון
3f	ברכת	ברכן

Imperfect

	Sing.	Plural
1	איבריך	נבריך
2m	תבריך	תברכון
2f	תברכין	תברכן
3m	יבריך	יברכון
3f	תבריך	יברכן

Participles

	Sing.	Plural
Masc.	מבריך	מברכין
Fem.	מברכה	מברכן

Imperative

Masc.	בריך
Fem.	ברכין
Plural	ברכון

Infinitive	למברכה

Transliteration:

Perfect

	Sing.	Plural
1	barrketh	barreknan
2m	barrekthah	barrekthun
2f	barrekth	barrektheyn
3m	barrek	barrekun
3f	barrkat	barrekan

Imperfect

	Sing.	Plural
1	eybarrek	nebarrek
2m	tebarrek	tebarrkun
2f	tebarrkhin	tebarrkan
3m	yebarrek	yebarrkun
3f	tebarrek	yebarrkan

Participles

	Sing.	Plural
Masc.	məbarrek	məbarrkin
Fem.	məbarrkah	məbarrkán

Imperative

Masc.	barrek
Fem.	barrkhin
Plural	barrkhun

| Infinitive | ləmbarrakah |

ETHPA'AL VERBS (איתברך) to Be Blessed

Perfect

	Sing.	Plural
1	איתברכית	איתברכנן
2m	איתברכת	איתברכתון
2f	איתברכת	איברכתין
3m	איתברך	איתברכון
3f	איתברכת	איתברכן

Imperfect

	Sing.	Plural
1	איתברך	נתברך
2m	תתברך	תתברכון
2f	תתברכין	תתברכן
3m	יתברכ	יתברכון
3f	תתברך	יתברכן

Participles

	Sing.	Plural
Masc.	מתברך	מתברכין
Fem.	מתברכה	מתברכן

Imperative

Masc.	איברך
Fem.	איברכין
Plural	איברכון

Infinitive   למתברכה

Transliteration:

Perfect

	Sing.	Plural
1	ithbarrketh	ithbarraknan
2m	ithbarrakth	ithbarrakthun
2f	ithbarrakth	ithbarraktheyn
3m	ithbarrak	ithbarrakun
3f	ithbarrkat	ithbarrakan

Imperfect

	Sing.	Plural
1	eythbarrak	nithbarrak
2m	tithbarrak	tithbarrkhun
2f	tithbarrkhin	tithbarrkhan
3m	yithbarrak	yithbarrkhun
3f	tithbarrak	yithbarrkhan

Participles

	Sing.	Plural
Masc.	mithbarrak	mithbarrkhin
Fem.	mithbarrkhah	mithbarrkhan

Imperative

Masc.	ithbarrak
Fem.	ithbarrkhin
Plural	ithbarrkhun

| Infinitive | ləmithbarrakhah |

APH'EL VERBS (אדביר) to Guide

Perfect

	Sing.	Plural
1	אדברית	אדבירנן
2m	אדבירת	אדבירתון
2f	אדבירת	אדבירתין
3m	אדביר	אדברון
3f	אדבירת	אדברן

Imperfect

	Sing.	Plural
1	אדביר	נדבר
2m	תדביר	תדברון
2f	תדברין	תדברן
3m	ידביר	ידברון
3f	תדביר	ידברן

Participles

	Sing.	Plural
Masc.	מדביר	מדברין
Fem.	מדברה	מדברן

Imperative

Masc.	אדביר
Fem.	אדברין
Plural	אדברון

| Infinitive | לֹמדברא |

Transliteration:

Perfect

	Sing.	Plural
1	adbreth	adbernan
2m	adberth	adberthun
2f	adberth	adbertheyn
3m	adber	adbrun
3f	adberat	adbran

Imperfect

	Sing.	Plural
1	adber	nadber
2m	tadber	tadbrun
2f	tadbrin	tadbran
3m	yadber	yadbrun
3f	tadber	yadbran

Participles

	Sing.	Plural
Masc.	madber	madbrin
Fem.	madbrah	madbran

Imperative

Masc.	adber
Fem.	adbrin
Plural	adbrun

Infinitive   ləmadbara

ETTAPH'AL VERBS (איתדבר) to Be Guided

Perfect

	Sing.	Plural
1	איתדברית	איתדברנן
2m	איתדברת	איתדברתון
2f	איתדברת	איתדברתין
3m	איתדבר	איתדברון
3f	איתדברת	איתדברן

Imperfect

	Sing.	Plural
1	איתדבר	נתדבר
2m	תתדבר	תתדברון
2f	תתדברין	תתדברן
3m	יתדבר	יתדברון
3f	תתדבר	יתדברן

Participles

	Sing.	Plural
Masc.	מתדבר	מתדברין
Fem.	מתדברה	מתדברן

Imperative

Masc.		איתדבר
Fem.		איתדברין
Plural		איתדברון

Infinitive		למתדברה

Transliteration:

Perfect

	Sing.	Plural
1	itadbreth	itadbarnan
2m	itadbarth	itadbarthun
2f	itadbarth	itadbartheyn
3m	itadbar	itadbrun
3f	itadbrath	itadbran

Imperfect

	Sing.	Plural
1	itadbar	nitadbar
2m	titadbar	titadbrun
2f	titadbrin	titadbran
3m	yitadbar	yitadbrun
3f	titadbar	yitadbran

Participles

	Sing.	Plural
Masc.	mitadbar	mitadbrin
Fem.	mitadbrá	mitadbrán

Imperative

Masc.	itadbar
Fem.	itadbrin
Plural	itadbrun

Infinitive   ləmitadbarah

PE-NUN VERBS (נפק) to Go Out

Perfect

	Sing.	Plural
1	נפקית	נפקנן
2m	נפקתה	נפקתון
2f	נפקת	נפקתין
3m	נפק	נפקון
3f	נפקת	נפקן

Imperfect

	Sing.	Plural
1	אפוק	נפוק
2m	תפוק	תפקון
2f	תפקין	תפקן
3m	יפוק	יפקון
3f	תפוק	יפקן

Participles

	Sing.	Plural
Masc.	נפק	נפקין
Fem.	נפקה	נפקן

Imperative

Masc.	פוק
Fem.	פוקין
Plural	פוקון

Infinitive	למפק

Transliteration:

Perfect

	Sing.	Plural
1	nefqeth	nəfaqnan
2m	nəfaqthah	nəfaqthun
2f	nəfaqth	nəfaqtheyn
3m	nəfaq	nəfqun
3f	nefqat	nəfqan

Imperfect

	Sing.	Plural
1	efuq	nifuq
2m	tifuq	tifqun
2f	tifqin	tifqan
3m	yifuq	yifqun
3f	tifuq	yifqan

Participles

	Sing.	Plural
Masc.	nafeq	nafqin
Fem.	nafqah	nafqán

Imperative

Masc.	fuq
Fem.	fuqin
Plural	fuqun

Infinitive   ləmefaq

NOTES FOR PE-NUN VERBS:

THE NUN AT THE BEGINNING OF THE WORD IS A WEAK
CONSONANT. NUN DISAPPEARS IN CERTAIN
CONJUGATIONS; ESPECIALLY THE IMPERFECT,
INFINITIVE, AND IMPERATIVE FORMS OF THE VERB.

WHEN THESE VERBS ARE USED TO FORM AN APH'EL
VERB, THE NUN DISAPPEARS AND IS REPLACED WITH
AN ALAP.

OTHERWISE, PE-NUN VERBS ARE CONJUGATED VERY
MUCH LIKE PE'AL VERBS.

PE-ALAPH VERBS (אכל) to Eat

Perfect

	Sing.	Plural
1	אכלית	אכלנ
2m	אכלתה	אכלתון
2f	אכלת	אכלתין
3m	אכל	אכלון
3f	אכלת	אכלן

Imperfect

	Sing.	Plural
1	איכול	נאכול
2m	תאכול	תאכלון
2f	תאכלין	תאכלן
3m	יאכול	יאכלון
3f	תאכול	יאכלן

Participles

	Sing.	Plural
Masc.	אכל	אכלין
Fem.	אכלה	אכלן

Imperative

Masc.	אכול
Fem.	אכולין
Plural	אכולון

Infinitive	למאכל

Transliteration:

Perfect

	Sing.	Plural
1	akhleth	akhalnan
2m	akhalthah	akhalthun
2f	akhalth	akhaltheyn
3m	akhal	akhlun
3f	akhlat	akhlan

Imperfect

	Sing.	Plural
1	ekhul	nekhul
2m	tekhul	tekhlun
2f	tekhlin	tekhlan
3m	yekhul	yekhlun
3f	tekhul	yekhlan

Participles

	Sing.	Plural
Masc.	akhel	akhlin
Fem.	akhlah	akhlán

Imperative

Masc.	akhul
Fem.	akhulin
Plural	akhulun

Infinitive   ləmekhal

NOTES: 'TO EAT' IS AN U-ROOT VERB. OTHER PE-ALAPH VERBS MAY MAINTAIN AN A-ROOT.

EX.

A-ROOT VERB:	אמר	[imar] to Say (he said)
IMPERFECT –	יימר	[yimar] He will say
IMPERATIVE –	אמר	[imar] Say!
INFINITIVE -	למאמר	[ləmimar] to Say

136

PE-YOD VERBS (ירת) to Inherit

Perfect

	Sing.	Plural
1	ירתית	ירתנן
2m	ירתתה	ירתתון
2f	ירתת	ירתתין
3m	ירת	ירתון
3f	ירתת	ירתן

Imperfect

	Sing.	Plural
1	איֿרת	ניֿרת
2m	תיֿרת	תיֿרתון
2f	תיֿרתין	תיֿרתן
3m	ייֿרת	ייֿרתון
3f	תיֿרת	ייֿרתן

Participles

	Sing.	Plural
Masc.	יריֿת	ירֿתין
Fem.	ירֿתה	ירֿתן

Imperative

Masc.	ירת	
Fem.	ירתין	
Plural	ירתון	

Infinitive   למירת

Transliteration:

Perfect

	Sing.	Plural
1	yərthet	yərethnan
2m	yərethtah	yərethtun
2f	yəretht	yərethteyn
3m	yəreth	yərethun
3f	yərthat	yərethan

Imperfect

	Sing.	Plural
1	ireth	nireth
2m	tireth	tirthun
2f	tirthin	tirthan
3m	yireth	yirthun
3f	tireth	yirthan

Participles

	Sing.	Plural
Masc.	yareth	yarthin
Fem.	yarthah	yarthán

Imperative

Masc.	yəreth
Fem.	yərethin
Plural	yərethun

Infinitive	ləmireth

NOTES: TWO IRREGULAR PE-YOD VERBS

	יתב [Yətev] to Sit	ידע [Yəda³] to Know
Perfect	יתב [Yətev]	ידע [Yəda³]
Imperf.	ייתיב [Yeytev]	יידע [Yeyda³]
Imperative	תיב [Teyv]	דע [Da³]
Infinitive	למיתב [Ləmeytev]	למידע [Ləmeyda³]
Participles	יתיב [Yatev]	ידיע [Yade³]

'E-ALAPH VERBS (שאל) to Ask

Perfect

	Sing.	Plural
1	שאלית	שאלנן
2m	שאלתה	שאלתון
2f	שאלת	שאלתין
3m	שאל	שאלון
3f	שאלת	שאלן

Imperfect

	Sing.	Plural
1	אישאל	נשאל
2m	תשאל	תשאלון
2f	תשאלין	תשאלן
3m	ישאל	ישאלון
3f	תשאל	ישאלן

Participles

	Sing.	Plural
Masc.	שאיל	שאלין
Fem.	שאלא	שאלן

Imperative

Masc.	שְׁאַל
Fem.	שַׁאֲלִין
Plural	שַׁאֲלוּן

Infinitive	לְמִשְׁאַל

Transliteration:

Perfect

	Sing.	Plural
1	she'let	she'lnan
2m	she'lthah	she'lthun
2f	she'lth	she'ltheyn
3m	she'l	she'lun
3f	she'lat	she'lan

Imperfect

	Sing.	Plural
1	eysha'l	nisha'l
2m	tisha'l	tishe'lun
2f	tishe'lin	tishe'lan
3m	yisha'l	yishe'lun
3f	tisha'l	yishe'lan

Participles

	Sing.	Plural
Masc.	sha'el	sha'lin
Fem.	sha'lah	sha'lán

Imperative

Masc.	sha'l
Fem.	sha'lin
Plural	sha'lun

Infinitive	ləmisha'l

HOLLOW VERBS (קוֹם) to Rise

Perfect

	Sing.	Plural
1	קמית	קמנן
2m	קמתה	קמתון
2f	קמת	קמתין
3m	קם	קמון
3f	קמת	קמן

Imperfect

	Sing.	Plural
1	איקום	נקום
2m	תקום	תקומון
2f	תקומין	תקומן
3m	יקום	יקומון
3f	תקום	יקומן

Participles

	Sing.	Plural
Masc.	קאים	קיימין
Fem.	קיימה	קיימן

Imperative

Masc.	קום
Fem.	קומין
Plural	קומון

Infinitive	למיקם

Transliteration:

Perfect

	Sing.	Plural
1	qameth	qamnan
2m	qamthah	qamthun
2f	qamth	qamtheyn
3m	qam	qamun
3f	qamath	qaman

Imperfect

	Sing.	Plural
1	equm	nequm
2m	tequm	tequmun
2f	tequmin	tequman
3m	yequm	yequmun
3f	tequm	yequman

Participles

	Sing.	Plural
Masc.	qa'em	qaymin
Fem.	qaymá	qaymán

Imperative

Masc.	qum
Fem.	qumin
Plural	qumun

Infinitive	ləmeqam

NOTES: TWO IRREGULAR HOLLOW VERBS

	מות [Mut] to Die	סום [Sum] to Put
Perfect	מית [Mit]	סם [Sam]
Imperf.	ימות [Yemut]	יסים [Yesim]
Imperative	מות [Mut]	סים [Sim]
Infinitive	למימת [Ləmemat]	למיסם [Ləmesam]
Participles	מאית [Ma'et]	סאים [Sa'em]

151

GEMINATE VERBS (עלל) to Enter

Perfect

	Sing.	Plural
1	עלית	עלْנ
2m	עלתא	עלתון
2f	עלת	עלתין
3m	עאל | עלל	עלון
3f	עלת	עלْן

Imperfect

	Sing.	Plural
1	אִיעוֹל	נֵעוֹל
2m	תֵעוֹל	תֵעֲלוֹן
2f	תִיעֲלִין	תֵעֲלָן
3m	יֵיעוֹל	יֵיעֲלוֹן
3f	תֵעוֹל	יֵיעֲלָן

Participles

	Sing.	Plural
Masc.	עֲלִיל	עֲלְלִין
Fem.	עֲלְלָה	עֲלְלָן

Imperative

Masc.	עול
Fem.	עולין
Plural	עולון

Infinitive	למיעול

Transliteration:

Perfect

	Sing.	Plural
1	ʻaleth	ʻalnan
2m	ʻaltha	ʻaltun
2f	ʻalth	ʻalteyn
3m	ʻal / ʻalal	ʻalun
3f	ʻalat	ʻalan

Imperfect

	Sing.	Plural
1	ey'ull	ne'ull
2m	te'ull	te'allun
2f	te'allin	te'allan
3m	yey'ull	ye'allun
3f	te'ull	ye'allan

Participles

	Sing.	Plural
Masc.	ʻaleyl	ʻallin
Fem.	ʻallah	ʻallán

Imperative

Masc.	ʻull
Fem.	ʻullin
Plural	ʻullun

| Infinitive | ləmeyʻull |

LAMAD-YOD #1 PE'AL ROOT (חמא) to See

Perfect

	Sing.	Plural
1	חמית	חמינן
2m	חמיתה	חמיתון
2f	חמית	חמיתין
3m	חמא	חמיון
3f	חמת	חמין

Imperfect

	Sing.	Plural
1	איחמי	נחמי
2m	תחמי	תחמון
2f	תחמין	תחמין
3m	יחמי	יחמון
3f	תחמי	יחמיין

Participles

	Sing.	Plural
Masc.	חמא	חמין
Fem.	חמיא	חמין

Imperative

Masc.	חמי
Fem.	חמיי
Plural	חמון

Infinitive	למחמא

Transliteration:

Perfect

	Sing.	Plural
1	Həmith	Həmaynan
2m	Həmaythah	Həmaythun
2f	Həmayth	Həmaytheyn
3m	Həmá	Həmiyun
3f	Həmath	Həmiyan

Imperfect

	Sing.	Plural
1	iHme	niHme
2m	tiHme	tiHmun
2f	tiHmayin	tiHmayán
3m	yiHme	yiHmun
3f	tiHme	yiHmayán

Participles

	Sing.	Plural
Masc.	Hame	Hameyn
Fem.	Hamyah	Hamyán

Imperative

Masc.	Həmey
Fem.	Həmay
Plural	Həmun

Infinitive	ləmeHme

LAMAD-YOD #2 PA'EL ROOT (צלי) to Pray

Perfect

	Sing.	Plural
1	צלּיית	צלּינן
2m	צלּיתה	צלּיתון
2f	צלּית	צלּיתין
3m	צלּי	צלּון
3f	צלּיית	צלּיין

Imperfect

	Sing.	Plural
1	איצלי	נצלי
2m	תצלי	תצלון
2f	תצליין	תצליין
3m	יצלי	יצלון
3f	תצלי	יצליין

Participles

	Sing.	Plural
Masc.	מצלי	מצליין
Fem.	מצלייא	מצלין

Imperative

Masc.	צְלִי
Fem.	צְלִיי
Plural	צְלוּן

Infinitive   לְמצלייה

Transliteration:

Perfect

	Sing.	Plural
1	tzalleyth	tzallinan
2m	tzallithah	tzallithun
2f	tzallith	tzallitheyn
3m	tzalli	tzallun
3f	tzallyath	tzallyan

Imperfect

	Sing.	Plural
1	etzalle	netzalle
2m	tetzalle	tetzallun
2f	tetzallyin	tetzallyan
3m	yetzalle	yetzallun
3f	tetzalle	yetzallyan

Participles

	Sing.	Plural
Masc.	mətzalley	mətzalleyn
Fem.	mətzallyah	mətzallyán

Imperative

Masc.	tzalley
Fem.	tzalláy
Plural	tzallun

Infinitive	ləmtzallayah

SHAPH'EL VERBS   (שעביד) to Subjugate

Perfect

	Sing.	Plural
1	שעבדית	שעבדנן
2m	שעבידתה	שעבדתון
2f	שעבידת	שעבדתין
3m	שעביד	שעבדון
3f	שעבדת	שעבדן

Imperfect

	Sing.	Plural
1	אשעביד	נשעביד
2m	תשעביד	תשעבדון
2f	תשעבדין	תשעבדן
3m	ישעביד	ישעבדון
3f	תשעביד	ישעבדן

Participles

	Sing.	Plural
Masc.	משעביד	משעבדין
Fem.	משעבדה	משעבדן

Imperative

Masc.	שעביד
Fem.	שעבדין
Plural	שעבדון

Infinitive	למשעבדה

Transliteration:

Perfect

	Sing.	Plural
1	sha'bdeth	sha'bednan
2m	sha'bedthah	sha'bedthun
2f	sha'bedth	sha'bedtheyn
3m	sha'bed	sha'bdun
3f	sha'bdat	sha'bdan

Imperfect

	Sing.	Plural
1	isha'bed	nesha'bed
2m	tesha'bed	tesha'bdun
2f	tesha'bdin	tesha'bdan
3m	yesha'bed	yesha'bdun
3f	tesha'bed	yesha'bdan

Participles

	Sing.	Plural
Masc.	məsha'bed	məsha'bdin
Fem.	məsha'bdah	məsha'bdan

Imperative

Masc.	sha'bed
Fem.	sha'bdin
Plural	sha'bdun

Infinitive	ləmsha'bdah

ESHTAPH'AL VERBS (אישתעביד) to Be Subjugated

Perfect

	Sing.	Plural
1	אישתעבדית	אישתעבידנן
2m	אישתעבידת	אישתעבדתון
2f	אישתעבידת	אישתעבדתין
3m	אישתעביד	אישתעבדון
3f	אישתעבדת	אישתעבדן

Imperfect

	Sing.	Plural
1	אשתעביד	נשתעביד
2m	תשתעביד	תשתעבדון
2f	תשתעבדין	תשתעבדן
3m	ישתעביד	ישתעבדון
3f	תשתעביד	ישתעבדן

Participles

	Sing.	Plural
Masc.	משתעביד	משתעבדין
Fem.	משתעבדה	משתעבדן

Imperative

Masc.	אישתעבד
Fem.	אישתעבדין
Plural	אישתעבדון

Infinitive	למשתעבדה

Transliteration:

Perfect

	Sing.	Plural
1	ishta'bdeth	ishta'badnan
2m	ishta'badth	ishta'badthun
2f	ishta'badth	ishta'badtheyn
3m	ishta'bad	ishta'bdun
3f	ishta'bdat	ishta'bdan

Imperfect

	Sing.	Plural
1	ishta'bad	nishta'bad
2m	tishta'bad	tishta'bdun
2f	tishta'bdin	tishta'bdan
3m	yishta'bad	yishta'bdun
3f	tishta'bad	yishta'bdan

Participles

	Sing.	Plural
Masc.	mishta'bad	mishta'bdin
Fem.	mishta'bdah	mishta'bdan

Imperative

Masc.	ishta'bad
Fem.	ishta'bdin
Plural	ishta'bdun

Infinitive   ləmishta'bdah

IRREGULAR VERB (אתא) to Come

Perfect

	Sing.	Plural
1	אתית	אתינן
2m	אתיתה	אתיתון
2f	אתית	אתיתין
3m	אתא	אתיון
3f	אתת	אתין

Imperfect

	Sing.	Plural
1	איתא	נאתא
2m	תאתא	תאתון
2f	תאתיין	תאתין
3m	יאתא	יאתון
3f	תאתא	יאתיין

Participles

	Sing.	Plural
Masc.	אתא	אתין
Fem.	אתיא	אתיין

Imperative

Masc.	תא
Fem.	תיי
Plural	תון

Infinitive	למיתא

Transliteration:

Perfect

	Sing.	Plural
1	athith	athinan
2m	atheythah	athithun
2f	atheyth	athitheyn
3m	atha	athiyun
3f	athath	athiyan

Imperfect

	Sing.	Plural
1	ithe	nithe
2m	tithe	tithun
2f	tithin	tithayan
3m	yithe	yithun
3f	tithe	yithayan

Participles

	Sing.	Plural
Masc.	athe	athin
Fem.	athyá	athyán

Imperative

Masc.	thá
Fem.	thay
Plural	thun

Infinitive   ləmeythá

APH'EL FORM OF VERB: TO BRING

Perf.	אייתי	[Aythi]
Imperf.	אייתי	[Yaythe]
Imp.	אייתי	[Aythi]
Inf.	למייתיה	[Ləmaythayah]

IRREGULAR VERB (אזל) to Go

Perfect

	Sing.	Plural
1	אזלית	אזלנן
2m	אזלתה	אזלתון
2f	אזלת	אזלתין
3m	אזל	אזלון
3f	אזלת	אזלן

Imperfect

	Sing.	Plural
1	אזל	נאזל
2m	תאזל	תאזלון
2f	תאזלין	תאזלן
3m	ייזל	ייזלון
3f	תאזל	ייזלן

Participles

	Sing.	Plural
Masc.	אזל	אזלין
Fem.	אזלה	אזלן

Imperative

Masc.	זיל
Fem.	זלין
Plural	זלון

Infinitive	למאזל | למיזל

Transliteration:

Perfect

	Sing.	Plural
1	azleth	azalnan
2m	azalthah	azalthun
2f	azalth	azaltheyn
3m	azal	azalun
3f	azlat	azalan

Imperfect

	Sing.	Plural
1	eyzel	nezel
2m	tezel	tezlun
2f	tezlin	tezlan
3m	yezel	yezlun
3f	tezel	yezlan

Participles

	Sing.	Plural
Masc.	azel	azlin
Fem.	azla	azlan

Imperative

Masc.	zel
Fem.	zlin
Plural	zlun

Infinitive	ləmezal

OTHER VERB FORMS:

An example of another verbal root form would be:

תרגם [TARGEM] TO TRANSLATE

*There is a small number of verbs that use a verbal stem such as this

PERFECT:

1	TARGƏMETH	TARGEMƏN
2	TARGEMTHAH	TARGEMTHON
	TARGEMTH	TARGEMTHEYN
3	TARGEM	TARGƏMUN
	TARGƏMATH	TARGƏMAN

IMPERFECT:

1	ATARGEM	NƏTARGEM
2	TƏTARGEM	TƏTARGƏMUN
	TƏTARGƏMIN	TƏTARGƏMAN
3	YƏTARGEM	YƏTARGƏMUN
	TƏTARGEM	YƏTARGƏMAN

PARTICIPLE:

    MƎTARGEM   MƎTARGƎMIN

    MƎTARGƎMAH   MƎTARGƎMÁN

IMPERATIVE:

    TARGEM! / TARGƎMIN! / TARGƎMUN!

HOLLOW VERBS BECOMING APH'EL VERBS:

Hollow Verb Stems replace the 'ו' with 'י' when creating the Causative Verbal Form (Aph'el).

Ex.   קוֹם   [Qum] to rise

         אקים   [Aqim] to lift

         רוֹם   [Rum] to be high

         ארים [Arim] to exalt

*Remember that Aph'el Verb Forms always start with 'א'

*The Passive Verbal Form of Hollow Verbs will also replace the 'ו' with 'י'

Ex.   לוֹט   [LuT] to curse

         איתליט [IthliT] to be cursed

ENCLITIC PRONOUNS AND PARTICIPLES:

This section will discuss the use of enclitic pronouns when they are used with participles. The following is a chart of enclitic pronouns:

Copulative [Enclitic] Pronouns

1	-בָא (Dep.) -NA	1st pers. sing.
2	-ת (Dep.) -AT	2nd pers. sing. Masc. / Fem.
3	------------------	3rd pers. sing. Masc. / Fem.
1	-בַן (Dep.) -NAN	1st pers. pl.
2	-תוּן (Dep.) -תִין (Dep.) -TUN -TEYN	2nd pers. pl. Masc. / Fem.
3	------------------	3rd pers. pl. Masc. / Fem.

*Enclitic particles are not used with third person sing m. / f. nor with third person plural m. / f.

PARTICIPLES: WITH VERB (כתב)

Masc.	כתיב KATEYV	'writing' 'writer'
Fem.	כתבה KATVAH	'writing' 'writer'
Masc. Pl.	כתבין KATVIN	'writing' 'writers'
Fem. Pl.	כתבן KATVAN	'writing' 'writers'

WITH ENCLITIC PRONOUNS:

*Enclitic Pronouns are combined with the Participle:

כתבנא   [Katev-ná] = I am writing

כתבת   [Katv-ath] = You are writing

Plural Participles are usually inflected as such:

כתבינן   [Katvi-nán] We are writing

כתביתון   [Katvi-tun] You are writing

*3rd Person Singular & Plural Participles do not receive an enclitic pronoun.

חזיא   [Hazey] = He sees

בעיא   [Ba'ey] = He wants

כתיב   [Kateyv] = He writes

כתבה   [Katvah] = She writes

חזין   [Hazin] = They see

The Perfect Tense Form of (הוה) 'to Be'

1	הוית	הוינן
2m	הויתה	הויתון
2f	הוית	הויתין
3m	הוה	הוון
3f	הות	הון

1	HƏWITH	HƏWAYNAN
2m	HƏWAYTHAH	HƏWAYTUN
2f	HƏWAYTH	HƏWAYTEYN
3m	HƏWAH	HƏWUN
3f	HƏWATH	HƏWAN

הוה [HƏVAH / HƏWAH] is used to create the continuative past with participles and past tense form of 'אית' (It).

Ex.

כתיב הוית

[Kateyv həwith] = I was writing

כתיבנא הוית

[Kateyv-na həwith] = I was writing (with enclitic part.)

כתבין הוינן

[Katvin həwaynan] = We were writing

...אית הוית לי

[Ith həwith li...] = I had...

*The conjugated verb 'הוה' must match the appropriate personal pronoun of the sentence.

ALTERNATIVE IMPERFECT TENSE CONJUGATIONS WITH 3RD PERSON VERBS

3	לכתוב ------ LIKHTUV	He will write	3rd pers. sing. Masc. Imperfect
3	לכתבון לכתבן LIKHTƏVUN LIKHTƏVAN	They will write	3rd pers. pl. Masc. / Fem. Imperfect

*The 3rd person sing. Feminine form is conjugated as it regularly is. Only imperfect verb conjugations with the 'ל' prefix are changed in some dialects.

*This is especially prevalent in Jewish Babylonian Aramaic and the Galilean dialect of Jewish Palestinian Aramaic.

TO BE ABLE TO, TO NEED & TO HAVE TO

The following constructions are used:

TO BE ABLE TO (CAN)

יָכֹל [Yəkhal] = to be able to

יָכִיל Yakheyl	יָכְלָה Yakhlah	יָכְלִין Yakhlin	יָכְלָן Yakhlán
Can (m.sing.)	Can (f.sing.)	Can (m.pl.)	Can (f.pl.)

These forms always have a participle that follows which matches the gender and number of this verb.

Ex.

אֲנָא יָכִיל עָבֵיד

[Ana yakheyl 'abed] = I can do [m.]

אֲנָא יָכְלָה אָזְלָה

[Ana yakhlah azlah] = I can go [f.]

אֲנַן יָכְלִין עָבְדִין

[Anan yakhlin 'abdin] = We can do [m.pl.]

TO NEED TO

צְרַךְ [Tzərakh] (verb) *conjugated normally and used as a participle that is followed by a infinitive verb* – to Need

צָרֵךְ [Tzarekh] (adjective) is used with the preposition (-לְ) - Necessity

Ex.

צְרִיכְנָא לְמֵיזַל

[Tzareykh-na ləmezal] = I need to go

צְרךְ לִי לְמֵיזַל

[Tzarekh li ləmezal] = I need to go

TO HAVE TO

אית ל- +   [It l- + (inf.) = I have to] *this construction is followed by an infinitive verb*

Ex.

אית לי למיזל

[It li ləmezal] = I have to go

FINAL NOTES ON VERBS:

1) The Verb 'to Come' is both PE-ALAPH & LAMAD YOD

2) APH'EL verbs must always begin with an Alap

3) When a verbal root begins with an Alap and appears as an APH'EL verb in the Glossary, the initial Alap of that verbal root will become a Yod with a Alap preceding it.

4) Remember that PE'AL verbs may have different root vowels in the Imperfect tense and the Imperative form. There are U-root, A-root and E-root verbs. All will be marked appropriately in the Glossary.

5) The imperfect tense sets the verb form for the Imperative minus the initial consonant.

6) Hollow Verbs will replace the Waw within their stem with a Yod when they are converted into a APH'EL verb

7) PE-NUN verbs always start with a NUN

8) PE-YOD verbs always start with an ALAP

XI) Negation

Negation is expressed very simply with the negative particle
(לֹא) [La]. There are some exceptions when the negative
particle is used in certain constructions.

לֹא

[La] = negative particle

General usage:

לֹא בעינא למיזל

[La ba'ey-na ləmezal] = I don't want to go [Participle]

לֹא ידיענא

[La yade'-na] = I don't know [Participle]

לֹא תאזל

[La tezel!] = Don't go! [Negative Command & Imperfect]

הוא לֹא אזל

[Hu la azal] = He did not go [Perfect]

With verb – There is /are…

לֹא + אִית

[La + It] = No (Not) + There is / are…

לֵית

[Leyt] = There is not… / There are not…

לֵית לִי מַיָּא

[Leyt li mayya] = I don't have water

לֵית לִי לְמֵיזֵל

[Leyt li ləmezal] = I do not have to go

XII) Imperatives

As was previously shown in Chapter X, verbs follow specific patterns. The following Chapter will be a rehash of the Imperative forms shown in Chapter X.

Also remember that despite the imperatives having endings that are written, they are not pronounced. There are some exceptions with Lamad-Yod verbs.

PE'AL

REGULAR: U-ROOT

כתב [Kətav] = to Write

כתוב! [Kətuv!] = Write! [m.]

כותבין! [Kutvin!] = Write! [f.]

כותבון! [Kutvun!] = Write! [m.pl.]

A-ROOT

דחל [DəHel] = to Be Afraid

דחל! [DəHal!] = Be Afraid! [m.]

דחלין! [DəHlin!] = Be Afraid! [f.]

דחלון! [DəHlun!] = Be Afraid! [m.pl.]

E-ROOT

עבד [ʻəbad] = To Do

עבד! [ʻəbed!] = Do! [m.]

עבדין! [ʻəbdin!] = Do! [f.]

עבדון! [ʻəbdun!] = Do! [m.pl.]

ETHPE'EL

איתקטיל [Ithqətel] = to Be Killed

איתקטיל! [Ithqətel!] = Be Killed! [m.]

איתקטלין! [Ithqətlin!] = Be Killed! [f.]

איתקטלון! [Ithqətlun!] = Be Killed! [m.pl.]

PA'EL

בריך [Barrek] = to Bless!

ברך! [Barrek!] = Bless! [m.]

ברכין! [Barrkhin!] = Bless! [f.]

ברכון! [Barrkhun!] = Bless! [m.pl.]

ETHPA'AL

איתברך [Ithbarrak] = to Be Blessed

איתברך! [Ithbarrak!] = Be Blessed! [m.]

איתברכין! [Ithbarrkhin!] = Be Blessed! [f.]

איתברכון! [Ithbarrkhun!] = Be Blessed! [m.pl.]

APH'EL

אדביר [Adber] = to Guide

אדביר! [Adber!] = Guide! [m.]

אדברין! [Adbrin!] = Guide! [f.]

אדברון! [Adbrun!] = Guide! [m.pl.]

ETTAPH'AL

איתדבר [Itadbar] = to Be Guided

איתדבר! [Itadbar!] = Be Guided! [m.]

איתדברין! [Itadbrin!] = Be Guided! [f.]

איתדברון! [Itadbrun!] = Be Guided! [m.pl.]

SHAPH'EL

שעביד [Sha'bed] = to Subjugate

שעביד! [Sha'bed!] = Subjugate! [m.]

שעבדין! [Sha'bdin!] = Subjugate! [f.]

שעבדון! [Sha'bdun!] = Subjugate! [m.pl.]

ESHTAPH'AL

אִישְׁתַּעֲבִיד [Ishtaʾbad] = to Be Subjugated

אִישְׁתַּעֲבִיד! [Ishtaʾbad!] = Be Subjugated! [m.]

אִישְׁתַּעֲבְדִין! [Ishtaʾbdin!] = Be Subjugated! [f.]

אִישְׁתַּעֲבְדוּן! [Ishtaʾbdun!] = Be Subjugated! [m.pl.]

PE-NUN

נְפַק [Nəfaq] = To Go Out

פּוּק! [Fuq!] = Go Out! [m.]

פּוּקִין! [Fuqin!] = Go Out! [f.]

פּוּקוּן! [Fuqun!] = Go Out! [m.pl.]

PE-ALAPH

U-ROOT

אכל [Akhal] = To Eat

אכול! [Akhul!] = Eat! [m.]

אכולין! [Akhulin!] = Eat! [f.]

אכולון! [Akhulun!] = Eat! [m.pl.]

A-ROOT

אמר [Imar] = to Say

אמר! [Imar!] = Say! [m.]

אמרין! [Imrin!] = Say! [f.]

אמרון! [Imrun!] = Say! [m.pl.]

PE-YOD

REGULAR

יֶרֶת [Yəreth] = to Inherit

יֶרַת! [Yərath!] = Inherit! [m.]

יֶרַתִין! [Yərathin!] = Inherit! [f.]

יֶרַתוּן! [Yərathun!] = Inherit! [m.pl.]

IRREGULAR

יְתִיב [Yətav] = to Sit

תִיב! [Tev!] = Sit! [m.]

תְבִין! [Təvin!] = Sit! [f.]

תְבוּן! [Təvun!] = Sit! [m.pl.]

יְדַע [Yəda'] = to Know

דַע! [Da'!] = Know! [m.]

דְעִין! [Da'in!] = Know! [f.]

דְעוּן! [Da'un!] = Know! [m.pl.]

NOTE: IRREGULAR VERB 'TO GIVE'

יְהַב   [Yəháv] Perfect Tense

הַב!   [Háv!] Give! (loses Yod)

'E-ALAPH

שאל [Sha'l] = to Ask

שאל! [Sha'l!] = Ask! [m.]

שאלין! [Sha'lin!] = Ask! [f.]

שאלון! [Sha'lun!] = Ask! [m.pl.]

HOLLOW ['E-WAW]

קום [Qum] = to Rise; Stand up

קום! [Qum!] = Rise! [m.]

קומין! [Qumin!] = Rise! [f.]

קומון! [Qumun!] = Rise! [m.pl.]

מית [Mit] = to Die

מות! [Mut!] = Die! [m.]

מותין! [Mutin!] = Die! [f.]

מותון! [Mutun!] = Die! [m.pl.]

GEMINATE

עלל [ʻAlal] = to Enter

עול! [ʻUll!] = Enter! [m.]

עולין! [ʻUllin!] = Enter! [f.]

עולון! [ʻUllun!] = Enter! [m.pl.]

LAMAD-YOD

PE'AL ROOT

חזא [Həza] = to See

!חזי [Hazey!] = See! [m.]

!חזיי [Hazay!] = See! [f.]

!חזון [Hazun!] = See! [m.pl.]

[WITH PA'EL ROOT]

צלי   [Tzalley] = to Pray

!צלי [Tzalley!] = Pray! [m.]

!צליי [Tzallay!] = Pray! [f.]

!צלון [Tzallun!] = Pray! [m.pl]

IRREGULAR IMPERATIVES

The verbs for 'to Go' and 'to Come' have irregular imperative forms.

אתא [Atha] = to Come

תא! [Thá!] = Come! [m.]

תיי! [Tháy!] = Come! [f.]

תון! [Thun!] = Come! [m.pl.]

אזל [Azal] = to Go

זיל! [Zel!] = Go! [m.]

זלין! [Zlin!] = Go! [f.]

זלון! [Zlun!] = Go! [m.pl.]

XIII) Imperatives with Negation

The only way to properly express a negative imperative in Aramaic is by using the 2nd person singular and plural imperfect forms. The negative particle will precede the verbal forms.

לֹא + [Lá] *negative particle*

תֵּאזֵל [Tezel] 2nd person Imperfect of 'To Go'

!לֹא תֵּאזֵל [Lá Tezel!] = Don't Go!

!לֹא תֵּאתֵא   [Lá Tithe!] = Don't Come!

!לֹא תֵּעְבְּדִיה   [Lá Teᵊbdeyh!] = Don't Do it!

!לֹא תִּיהֵב לֵיה לַחְמָא

[Lá Tihav leyh laHmá!] = Don't give him the Bread!

!לֹא תֵּקְטְלַנִי   [Lá Teqtlani!] = Don't kill me!

XIV) Pronominal Suffixes attached to Verbs

This final chapter of the Grammar Section will cover Pronominal Suffixes as Objects when a Perfect Tense verb or Imperfect Tense verb is involved. These Pronominal Suffixes for the most part can be used with Perfect, Imperfect and some Participles and Imperatives. Many imperatives will use the indirect object particle (-לְ) [which implies the meaning 'to me, to you'], but many others will use these same pronominal suffixes. The following chart will show objective pronominal suffixes connected with the verb for 'to Kill'

Accusative Pronominal Suffixes

1	‏-נִי‬ ‏-ן‬ -ni -an	1st pers. sing.
2	‏-ךָ‬ ‏-יךְ‬ -akh -eykh	2nd pers. sing. Masc. / Fem.
3	‏-יהָ‬ -eyh ‏-הֵ‬ -eh ‏-הָ‬ -ah	3rd pers. sing. Masc. / Fem.
1	‏-נַן‬ ‏-ן‬ -nan -an	1st pers. pl.
2	‏-כּוּן‬ ‏-כִּין‬ -khun -akhun -khin -akhin	2nd pers. pl. Masc. / Fem.
3	‏-(ה)וּן‬ ‏-(ה)ִין‬ -hun / -un -hin / -in	3rd pers. pl. Masc. / Fem.

קְטַל [Qtal; Qətal] to Kill

The Basic perfect roots that will be used with the following chart:

	Sing.	Plural
1	קטלת-	קטלנ-
2m	קטלת-	קטלתונ-
2f	קטלת-	קטלתינ-
3m	קטל-	קטלונ-
3f	קטלת-	קטלנ-

Transliteration:

Sing.		Plural
1	*Qtalt-	Qtaln-
2m	Qtalt-	Qtaltun-
2f	Qtalt-	Qtalteyn-
3m	Qatl-	Qatlun-
3f	Qtalt-	Qatlan-

*Usually, the 1st person singular Perfect form is: Qetlet

Singular Perfect Verb

Obj.	3m	3f	2m	2f	1
No suffix	קטל	קטלת	קטלת	קטלת	קטלית
1	קטלי	קטלני	קטלתני	קטלני	
2m	קטלך	קטלתך			קטלתך
2f	קטליך	קטלתיך			קטלתיך
3m	*קטליה*	*קטלתיה*	*קטלתינה*	*קטלתינה*	קטלתיה
3f	*קטלה*	*קטלתה*	*קטלתינה*	*קטלתינה*	**קטלתה**
1pl	קטלן	קטלתן	קטלתינן	קטלינן	
2mpl	קטלכון	קטלתכון			**קטלתכון**
2fpl	**קטלכין**	**קטלתכין**			**קטלתכין**

	1 sing	2m sing	3m sing	3f sing	3m pl
3m pl	**קטלתנון**	**קטלתינון**	**קטלון**	**קטלתון**	**קטלונון**

*The third person plural suffix loses 'ה' with most conjugations of the perfect tense

Transliteration:

Singular Perfect Verb

Obj.	3m	3f	2m	2f	1
No suffix	qtal	qatlat	qtalt	qtalt	qetlet
1	qatli	qtalatni	qtaltani	qtaltani	
2m	qatlak	qtaltak			qtaltak
2f	qatlik	qtaltik			qtaltik
3m	qatleyh	qtalteyh	qtaltineh	qtaltineh	qtalteyh
3f	qatlah	qtaltah	qtaltinah	qtaltinah	qtaltah
1pl	qatlan	qatlatan	qtaltinan	qtaltinan	
2mpl	qtalkhun	qatlakhun			qtaltakhun
2fpl	qtalkhin	qatlakhin			qtaltakhin

	1 sing	2m sing	3m sing	3f sing	3m pl
3m pl	qtaltinun	qtaltinun	qatlun	qtaltun	qatlunun

*The third person plural suffix loses 'ה' with most conjugations of the perfect tense

Plural Perfect Verb

Obj.	3mpl	3fpl	2mpl	2fpl	1pl
No suffix	קטלון	קטלן*	קטלתון	קטלתין	קטלנן
1	קטלוני		קטלתוני	קטלתיני	
2m	קטלונך				קטלנתך
2f	קטלוניך				קטלנתיך
3m	קטלונה		קטלתונה קטלתונה		קטלנתה
3f	קטלונה		קטלתינה קטלתינה		קטלנתה
1pl	קטלונן		קטלתונן קטלתינן		
2mpl	קטלונכון				קטלנכון
2fpl	קטלונכין				קטלנכין

*3fpl carries the accusative pronominal suffix in the same manner that 3mpl does. The only difference is that 3fpl does not have a 'ן'

221

Transliteration:

Plural Perfect Verb

Obj.	3mpl	3fpl	2mpl	2fpl	1pl
No suffix	qtalun	qtalan	qtaltun	qtaltin	qtalnan
1	qatluni		qtaltuni	qtaltini	
2m	qatlunak				qtalnatak
2f	qtalunik				qtalnatik
3m	qatluneh		qtaltuneh	qtaltinah	qtalnateh
3f	qatlunah		qtaltunah	qtaltinah	qtalnatah
1pl	qatlunan		qtaltunan	qtaltinan	
2mpl	qatlunakhun				qtalnakhun
2fpl	qatlunakhin				qtalnakhin

With Imperfect

	3m	2f	3mpl	3fpl
no suffix	יקטול	תקטלין	יקטלון	יקטלן
1st	יקטליני	תקתלינני	יקטלונני	יקטלנני
2m	יקטלינך		יקטלונך	יקטלנך
2f	יקטליניך		יקטלוניך	יקטלניך
3m	יקטליניה	תקטליניה	יקטלוניה	יקטלניה
3f	יקטלינה	תקטלינה	יקטלונה	יקטלנה
1pl	יקטלינן	תקטלינן	יקטלונן	יקטלנן
2mpl	**יקטלינכון**		יקטלונכון	יקטלנכון
2fpl	יקטולינכין		יקטלונכין	יקטלנכין

	3m sing	3m pl
3m pl	יקטלינון	יקטלונון

*The third person plural suffix usually drops the 'ה' when used with most imperfect conjugations

223

Transliteration:

With Imperfect

	3m		2f	3mpl	3fpl
no suffix	yiqtul	teqtlin		yiqtlun	yiqtlán
1st	yiqtlini	teqtlináni		yiqtlunáni	yiqtlanáni
2m	yiqtlinak			yiqtlunak	yiqtlanak
2f	yiqtlinikh			yiqtlunek	yiqtlanek
3m	yiqtlineyh	teqtlineyh		yiqtluneyh	yiqtlaneyh
3f	yiqtlináh	teqtlináh		yiqtlunah	yiqtlanah
1pl	yiqtlinán	teqtlinán		yiqtlunán	yiqtlanán
2mpl	yiqtlinakhun			yiqtlunakhun	yiqtlanakhun
2fpl	yiqtlinakhin			yiqtlunakhin	yiqtlanakhin

	3m sing	3m pl
3m pl	yiqtlinun	yiqtlunun

*The third person plural suffix usually drops the 'ה' when used with most imperfect conjugations

224

With Imperatives

Singular verb

	m.	f.
1st	קטלי	קטליני
3m	קטליה	קטלינה
3f	קטלה	קטלינה
1pl	קטלן	קטלינן

Plural verb

Short form

	m.	f.
1st	קטלוני	קטלני
3m	קטלוניה	קטלניה
3f	קטלונה	קטלנה
1pl	קטלונן	קטלנן

Transliteration:

With Imperatives

Singular verb

Obj.

	m.	f.
1st	QITLI	QITLINI
3m	QITLEYH	QITLINEH
3f	QITLAH	QITLINAH
1pl	QITLAN	QITLINAN

Plural verb

Short form

Obj.

	m.	f.
1st	QITLUNI	QITLÁNI
3m	QITLUNEYH	QITLÁNEYH
3f	QITLUNAH	QITLÁNAH
1pl	QITLUNAN	QITLÁNAN

Pronominal Suffixes with the Masculine Participle:

עביד ['ABED] MAKES (MASC. PARTICIPLE)

1st sing.	עבדיני 'ABDINI	It makes me
2nd sing.	עבדך עבדיך 'ABDAKH 'ABDIKH	It makes you
3rd sing.	עבדיה עבדה 'ABDEYH 'ABDAH	It makes him / her
1st pl.	עבדנן 'ABEDNAN	It makes us
2nd pl.	עבדכון 'ABEDKHUN	It makes you all
3rd pl.	עבדינון 'ABDINUN	It makes them

Part II

I)   English – Aramaic Glossary

Abbreviations used in this Glossary:

m. = masculine

f. = feminine

Adj. = Adjective

Pl. = Plural

Pe. = Pe'al verb form

Pa. = Pa'el verb form

Aph. = Aph'el verb form

NOTE: The majority of the verbs have the Pə'al verb form unless otherwise indicated

A

ABLE TO

אשכח   [AshkaH]

יכל   [Yəkhal]

ALSO

אוף   ['Of]

אף   [Af]

ANGEL

מלאכא   [Mal'akha]

אראל   [Er'el]

ANSWER

ענא   ['Ana]

ANYTHING

כלום   [Klum]

ASHES

קטמא   [QiTmá]

ASK

בעא   [Bə'a]

שאל   [Shə'al]

AUTHOR

כתיב   [Kateyv]

B

BE

הוא   [Hava / Hawa]

BELIEVE

הימין   [Heymeyn]

BLACK, BE

שחר   [ShəHar]

BLASPHEME

גדיף   [Gaddeyf] pa.

BLESS

ברך   [Barrek] pa.

BLESSING

ברכתא   [Birkhtha]

BLOOD

אדמא   [Adma]

BODY

גופא [Gufa]

BOY

טליא [Talyá]

תינוק [Thinoq]

רביא [Ravyá]

BREAD

לחמא [LaHma]

BRING

אייתי [Ayti] aph.

BROTHER

אחא [AHa]

BUILD

בנא [Bəna]

BUY

זבן [Zəvan]

C

CAESAR

קיסר [Qeysar]

CALF [animal]

תורתא [Thorthá]

CAPPADOCIA

קפדוקיא [Qapduqyá]

CHEESE

גובנא [Guvna]

CLOTHE

לבש [Ləvash]

COME

אתא [Atha]

CREATE

ברא [Bəra]

CROSS [noun]

צליבא [Tzəliva]

CROSS [verb]

עבר ['Əbar]

CURE

אסי [Assey]

D

DATE [fruit]

תמרא   [Thámrá]

DAUGHTER

ברתא   [Bəratha]

DAY

יומא   [Yoma]

DEATH

מותא   [Motha]

דמכותא   [Damkhuthá]

DEMON

שדא   [Sheyda]

מזיק   [Maziq]

DEPOSIT

פקד   [Fəqad]

DESIRE [verb]

רגג   [Rəgag]

תאב   [Thə'ev]

DESPISE

בזא   [Bəzá]

DIE

מית   [Mit] *Hollow root verb*

DIVIDE

פלג   [Fəlag]

DO

עבד   ['Abad]

DOG

כלבא   [Kalba]

DONKEY

חמרא   [Hamara]

DOVE

יונא   [Yona] *absolute state*

יונתא   [Yonthá] *emphatic state*

DREAM [verb]

חלם   [Halam]

DRINK

שתא   [Shətha]

DRY, BE

נגב   [Nəgev]

DRY, BECOME

נגב   [Nəgev]

E

EAT

אכל [Akhal]

EGYPT

מצרין [Mitzrayin]

ENTER

עלל ['Alal]

EVIL [adj.]

ביש [Bish]

EVIL ONE, THE

בישא [Bishá]

EXCREMENT

צואה [Tzo'ah] *absolute state*

EYE

עיינא ['Ayna]

F

FAST [verb]

צום   [Tzum] *Hollow root verb*

FATHER

אבא   [Aba]

FEAR

דחל   [DəHel]

FIELD

חלקא   [Helqa]

FIG

תאנתא   [Tə'eyntha]

FIRE

אשתא [Eshatha]

נורא [Nora]

FRUIT

פורא [Porá]

G

GARDEN

גינתא   [Gintha]

GIRL

טליתא   [Talithá]

GIVE

יהב   [Yəhav] *all tenses*

נתן   [Nəthan] *imperfect and infinitive only*

GO

אזל   [Azal]

GOAT

עזא   ['Iza]

GOD

אלה   [Elah] *absolute state*

אלהא   [Eláhá] *emphatic state*

GO DOWN

נחת   [NəHat]

GOOD [adj.]

טב   [Tav]

GO OUT

נפק   [Nəfaq]

GO UP

סלק   [Səleq]

H

HEAL

אסי   [Assey]

HEAR

שמע   [Shəma']

HEAVEN

שמיא   [Shəmaya]

HEIFER

תורתא   [Thorthá]

HERE

כא   [Kha']

הכא   [Hakha]

כאן   [Ka'n / Ka'an]

HOLY

קדוש   [Qadosh]

HOLY SPIRIT

רוחא דקודשא [RuHa dəQodsha]

HONEY

דובשא [Duvsha]

HOUSE

ביתא [Bayta]

J

JACKAL

תעלא   [Tha'alá]

JOIN

לוי   [Ləwey]

K

KILL

קטל   [QəTal]

KING

מלכא   [Malka]

KINGDOM

מלכותא   [Malkuta]

KNIFE

איזמיל   [Izmeyl]

סכין   [Sakin]

KNOW

ידע   [Yəda']

L

LABOR [verb]

פְּעַל   [Pə'al]

LAMB

אִמְרָא   [Imra]

LAND

אַרְעָא   [Ar'a]

LEARN

יְלַף   [Yəlaf]

תְּנָא   [Təna]

אֲלַף   [Alaf]

LIFE

חַיָּא   [Hayya]

LION

אַרְיָא   [Arya]

LIVE [verb]

חיא   [Həya]

קים   [Qim]

LOOK

אודיק   ['Odiq] aph.

סכא   [Səkhá]

צפא   [Tzəfá]

LOST, BE

אבד   [Abad]

LOVE [noun]

חובא   [Huba]

LOVE [verb]

רחם   [RəHem]

M

MAKE

עבד   ['Abad]

MAN

אינשא   [Inshá]

גוברא   [Guvrá]

גברא   [Gavrá]

MEAT

בשרא   [Bisrá]

קופדא   [Qufdá]

MELON

אבטיחא   [AvTiHa]

MILK

חלבא   [Halva]

MONEY

ממונא [Mamona]

MOTHER

אמא [Ima]

MOUNTAIN

טורא [Torá]

MOURN

אביל [Aveyl]

MOURNER

אביל [Aveyl]

MUST [auxiliary]

צריך [Tzareykh] *participle*

N

NAME

שמא   [Shəma]

NECESSITY

צרך   [Tzarekh] adj.

NECK

ענקא   ['Inqa]

NEED [verb]

צרך   [Tzərakh]

NIGHT

ליליא   [Leylya]

NOTHING

אין   [Eyn]

O

OLIVE

זיתא   [Zayta]

OPEN

פתח   [FətaH]

OX

תורא   [Thorá]

P

PEACE

שלמא   [Shlama]

PLACE [noun]

אתרא   [Atra]

POMEGRANATE

רומנתא   [Rumánthá]

PRAY

צלי   [Tzalley] pa.

PROPHET

נביא   [Nəviya]

PURE, BE

דכא   [Dəkha]

PUT

שם   [Sam]

Q

QUEEN

מלכתא   [Malktha]

QUIET, BE

שתק   [Shətaq]

R

RAM [animal]

אֵיל [Ayil]

READ

קְרָא [Qəra]

RECEIVE

קַבֵּל [Qabbel] pa.

שְׁקַל [Shəqal] pe.

RECITE

תְּנָא [Təna]

RECKON

חֲשַׁב [Həshav]

REMOVE

סַלֵּק [Salleq]

REQUEST

בעא   [Bə'a]

REQUIRE

בעא   [Bə'a]

RESEMBLE

דמא   [Dəma]

RETURN

הדר   [Hadar]

תוב   [Tuv]

REVEAL

גלא   [Gəla]

RICHES

ממונא   [Mamona]

RISE

קום   [Qum] *Hollow root verb*

RUN

רחט [RəHaT]

פרא [Pərá]

S

SANCTIFIED, BE

אתקדש   [Ithqadash]

SANCTIFY

קדיש   [Qaddeysh] pa.

SAY

אמר   [Imar]

SALT

מלחא   [MilHa]

SEE

חזא   [Həza]

חמא   [Həmá]

SEEK

בעא   [Bə'a]

תבע   [Thəva']

SELL

זבין   [Zavveyn] pa.

SILENT, BE

שתק   [Shətaq]

SIT

יתב   [Yətav]

SKULL

גולגלתא   [Gulgultha]

SLAUGHTER

דבח   [DəbaH] pe.

דבח   [DabbeH] pa.

SOMETHING

כלום   [Klum]

SON

ברא   [Bəra]

SOUL

נפשא   [Nafsha]

SPEAK

מלל   [Mallel] pa.

STAND

קום   [Qum] *Hollow root verb*

STATE

מדינתא   [Mədintha]

STILL

אדיין   [Adayin]

STONE

אבנא   [Abna]

כיפא   [Keyfá]

SUN

שמשא   [Shimshá]

שימשא   [Shimshá]

T

TAKE

שְׁקַל   [Shəqal]

קְנָא   [Qəná]

TAKE AWAY

נְסַב   [Nəsav]

TEACH

תְּנָא   [Təna]

יְלַף   [Yəlaf]

TELL

אֲמַר   [Imar]

THAT [conj.]

דְּ-   [Də-]

THERE

תמן   [Thamán]

הלן   [Halán]

THERE IS / ARE

אית   [It]

THERE IS / ARE NOT

לית   [Leyt]

THINK

חשב   [Həshav]

THIS

האי   [Hay]

הא   [Ha]

הני   [Haney]

THROW

רמא   [Rəmá]

TIME

זימנא   [Zimna]

TONGUE

לשנא   [Lishana]

TOO

אוף   ['Of]

אף   [Af]

TREE

אילנא   [Ilana]

W

WALK

הליך   [Halleykh] pa.

WANT

בעא   [Bə'a]

רגג   [Rəgag]

תאב   [Thə'ev]

WATER

מייא   [Mayya]

WEALTH

ממונא   [Mamona]

WEEP

דמע   [Dəma]

בכא   [Bəkha]

WHAT?

מאי [Mai]

מה [Mah]

מא [Ma]

WHERE?

האן [Ha'an]

אן [An]

WHY?

למה [Ləmah]

WIDOW

ארמלא [Armla]

WINE

חמרא [Hamra]

WISDOM

חוכמתא [Hokhmətha]

WOMAN

אִיתָא   [Itha]

אַתְתָא   [It-tha]

WORD

מִילְתָא   [Meyltha]

WORDS

מִילִי   [Meyley] pl. noun (*absolute state*)

מִילִיא   [Meláyá] pl. noun (*emphatic state*)

WORLD

עָלְמָא   ['Alma]

WRITE

כְתַב   [Kətav]

WRITER

כָתִיב   [Kateyv]

WRITING

כְתַבְתָא   [Kəthavtha]

Y

YEAR

שׁנא   [Shəna] *absolute state*

שׁנתא   [Shanthá] *emphatic state*

שׁתא   [Shathá] *emphatic state*

YET

אדיין   [Adayin]

YOU

אנת   [Ant] (m. & f. sing.)

את   [At] (m. & f. sing.)

אתון   [Atun] (m.pl)

אתין   [Ateyn] (f.pl.)

II)   Aramaic – English Glossary

Abbreviations used in this section:

(o) verb with 'o' root in imperfect   abs. = absolute

(e) verb with 'e' root in imperfect   constr. = construct

(a) verb with 'a' root in imperfect

[m.] = masculine   (ettaph.) = ETTAPH'AL VERB

[f.] = feminine

[pl.] = plural

[m.pl.] = masculine plural

[f.pl.] = feminine plural

(pe.) = PE'AL VERB

(ethp.) = ETHPE'EL VERB

(pa.) = PA'EL VERB

(ethpa.) = ETHPA'AL VERB

(aph.) = APH'EL VERB

(shaph.) = SHAPH'EL VERB

(n.) = Noun

(adj.) = Adjective

NOTE: Some nouns within this Glossary may be in the absolute state, while the majority of the nouns will primarily be in the emphatic state.

א

אבא

[Abá] = Father

אבד

[Abad] = [verb] to perish, be lost (a); to destroy, to lose (aph.)

אבטיחא

[AvTiHá] = Melon (m.)

אבל (אביל)

[Abeyl] = (verb) to mourn

אביל

[Abeyl] = Mourner

אבנא

[Abná] = Stone (f.)

אֲגַר

[Agar] = (verb) to hire

אַגְרָא

[Agrá] = wages

אֲדַיִן

[Adayin] = yet; still (adv.)

אַדְמָא

[Admá] = blood (m.)

אִדְרָא

[Idrá] = skin; hide

אַדְרַע

[Edra'] = arm (f.)

אוֹ

[O] = or

אוֹדִיק

[Odiq] = (aph'el verb) to look

אוּדְנָא

[Udná] = ear (f.)

אוכם

[Ukham] = black (adj.)

אולפן

[Ulfan] = doctrine (m.)

אומא

[Umá] = a people; nation

אומייא

[Umayyá] = peoples; nations

אומן

[Uman] = artisan (m.)

אומנו

[Umanu] = trade (f.)

אוף

['Of] = too, also

אוצר

[Otzar] = treasury; granary (m.)

אזא

[Aza] = to make hot; to heat

אָזַל

[Azal] = [verb] to go (e)

אַחָא

[AHá] = Brother

אַחוֹנִייָא

[AHwaniyyá] = plums

אַחַת

[AHat] = Sister

אִיגְרָא

[Igárá] = roof (m.)

אִיוָא

[Iwwá] = thorn (m.)

אִיזְמִיל

[Izmeyl] = knife (m.)

אַיִל

[Ayil] = ram (m.)

אִילָנָא

[Iláná] = tree

אילפא

[Ilpá] = ship (f.)

אימא

[Imá] = mother (f.)

אימה

[Eymah] = fear; awe (f.)

איממא

[Imámá] = day-time

אימר

[Imar] = lamb (m.)

אין

[In] = if

אין

[Eyn] = nothing

אינשא

[Inshá] = man (m.)

איסרטא

[IsraTá] = street

אִיקָרָא

[Iqárá] = honor

אִית

[It] = there is / are…

אִיתְתָא

[It-thá] = woman; wife (f.)

אִיתְמָל

[Itmál] = yesterday

אָכֵין

[Akheyn] = thus

אָכַל

[Akhal] = [verb] to eat, consume (u)

אַכְסַנְיָא

[Akhsenyá] = stranger; beggar

אֶלָא

[Ela] = but (conj.); unless

אֱלָהָא

[Eláhá] = God

אִלּוּ

[Ilo] = if [contrary to fact]

אֶלֶף

[Álaf] = one thousand

אֶלֶף

[Alaf] = [verb] to learn; practice (pe.); to teach (pa.)

אִמָּא

[Imma] = mother

אָמַר

[Imar] = [verb] to say (a)

אָן

[An] = where?

אֲנָא

[Ana] = I

אנדרטא

[AndráTá] = statue

אַנְת

[Ant] = You [m.]

אסא

[Asa] = to be healthy (pe.); to heal (pa.); to be healed (ithpa.)

אסטלא

[STlá] = garment (f.) *silent initial aleph*

אסטרטא

[IsTraTá] = street

אסר

[Esar] = [verb] to bind (o)

אף

[Af] = also, even

אפא

[Apá] = face (m.)

אפא

[Apa] = to bake

אפיקרסין

[Apiqarsin] = underwear

אראל

[Er'el] = angel (m.)

ארגוון

[Argwán] = purple (adj.)

ארחא

[ArHá] = traveller

אריא

[Aryá] = lion (m.)

ארמאי

[Armay] = Roman; pagan (n.)

ארמלתא

[Armǝltha] = widow

ארסא

[Irsá] = poison (m.)

ארע

[Ara'] = to meet (pe.); to be met (ithpe.)

ארעא

[Ar'á] = land

ארעתא

[Ar'átha] = lands [pl.]

אשכח

[AshkaH] = [verb] to find, to be able

אשפלא

[Ashplá] = basket (f)

אשתא

[Eshthá] = fire (f.)

את

[At] = you (m. & f.)

אתא

[Atha] = [verb] to come; (aph.) to bring

אתבונן

[Ithbonen] = to understand

אתין

[Ateyn] = you all (f.)

אתון

[Atun] = you all (m.)

אתרא

[Atrá] = place [m.]

אתרוותא

[Atrawáthá] = places [pl.]

ב

-ב

[B-] = in, by, with

באש

[B'esh] = [verb] to be bad (a); (aph.) to do evil

בבל

[Babel] = Babylon

-בגין ד

[Bəgin də-] = in order that

-בדיל ד

[Bidil də-] = because (conj.)

בהת

[Bəhat] = [verb] to be ashamed (a)

בוכרא

[Bukhrá] = firstborn (m.)

בוֹצִין

[Botzin] = lamp (m.)

בְזָא

[Bəzá] = to despise (pe.); to disgrace (pa.); to quarrel (ithpe.)

בְזַז

[Bəzaz] = [verb] to plunder (o)

בַזְבֵז

[Bazbez] = to squander

בִזְיוֹנָא

[Bizyoná] = disgrace (m.)

בְחַר

[BəHar] = to pick out, choose

בְחִיר

[BəHir] = chosen; elect (adj.)

בִיוָא

[Biwwá] = breast (m.)

ביוייא

[Biwwayyá] = breasts (m.pl.)

בין

[Bin] = to discern; (pa.) to cause to know

בין

[Beyn] = between (prep.)

ביעא

[Bey'á] = egg (m.)

בירתא

[Birtha] = fortress; palace

בישא

[Bisha] = the Evil One

ביש

[Bish] = evil [adj.]

ביתא

[Baythá] = house

בכא

[Bəkhá] = to cry; weep

בלא

[Bəlá] = without (prep.)

בלבד

[Bilbad] = only (conj.)

בלבל

[Balbel] = to confuse [verb]

בלחוד

[BelHod] = alone

בנא

[Bəná] = [verb] to build

בנאי

[Banay] = builder

בעא

[Bə'á] = [verb] to ask for, seek, require; want

בעט

[Bə'aT] = to kick

בעלא

[Ba'alá] = husband

בְּעַר

[Bə'ar] = to burn

בַּקֵּר

[Baqqer] = to search; investigate

בְּרָא

[Bərá] = son

בְּרָא

[Bərá] = [verb] to create

בְּרִייָא

[Barəyá] = creator

בְּרִיָא

[Biryá] = creature (f.)

בְּרִיךְ

[Brikh] = blessed [adj.]

בְּרֵךְ

[Barrek] = [verb] to bless (pa.)

בִּרְכְּתָא

[Birkthá] = blessing

ברר

[Bərar] = to purify

בריר

[Bərir] = clean, innocent (adj.)

ברתא

[Bartha] = daughter

בשרא

[Bisrá] = meat (m.)

בתר

[Bátar] = after

ג

גאא

[Gə'á] = to be high; proud (pe.); to boast (ithpa.)

גאל

[Gə'ál] = to ransom; redeem

גואל

[Go'el] = redeemer

גאולה

[Gə'ulah] = redemption (f.)

גב (גבי)

[Gav (Gavey)] = within

גבא

[Gəbá] = [verb] to collect taxes or debts

גבאי

[Gabbay] = a tax gatherer (m.)

גבב

[Gəvav] = to gather flowers

גבר

[Gəvar] = to be strong; to prevail

גוברא

[Guvrá] = man

גדא

[Gadá] = Destiny; Divinity

גדול

[Gadol] = great (adj.)

גדיא

[Gadyá] = kid (m.)

גדיף

[Gaddef] = [verb] to blaspheme (pa.)

גו

[Go] = within (prep.)

גוב

[Guv] = the body

גובאי

[Guvay] = locust (m.)

גובנא

[Guvná] = cheese (m.)

גוון

[Gawán] = sort, kind

גוגלתא

[Gulgulthá] = skull (f.)

גוף

[Guf] = to embrace [*hollow root verb*]

גופא

[Gufá] = body (m.)

גזא

[Gazá] = treasure (m.)

גזורתא

[Gəzurthá] = circumcision

גזר

[Gəzar] = to have oneself circumcised

גחך

[GəHakh] = to laugh (pe.); to mock (pa.)

גטא

[GiTá] = document (m.)

גיהנם

[Geyhinam] = Hell, Gehenna

גינתא

[Gintha] = garden [f.]

גיפא

[Geyfá] = sea-shore; river bank

גלא

[Gəlá] = to reveal oneself (pe.); to banish (aph.)

גלגל

[Galgel] = wheel (m.)

גלותא

[Galuthá] = exile; captivity (f.)

גלילא

[Galili] = Galilee

גמל

[Gəmal] = to requite, repay; show mercy

גמלא

[Gamlá] = camel (m.)

גמר

[Gəmar] = to finish; bring to an end

גנא

[Giná] = garden (m.)

גנא

[Gəná] = to act disgracefully

גנב

[Gənav] = to steal

גער

[Gə'ar] = to rebuke; scold

גרא

[Gərá] = to sue; contend with

גרמא

[Garmá] = bone (m.)

גריש

[Gareysh] = [verb] to drag (pa.)

ד

‑ד

[Də‑] = of, which, that, who

דבורא

[Dəvorá] = bee (f.)

דבוריא

[Dəvoryá] = beehive (f.)

דביח

[DabbeH] = [verb] to sacrifice (pa.)

דבחתא

[DibHəthá] = sacrifice [f.]

דבר

[Dəbar] = [verb] to lead (a); (pa.) to govern; (aph.) to guide

דהבא

[Dahabá] = gold

דובשא

[Duvshá] = honey

דודא

[Dodá] = friend; uncle

דור

[Dor] = generation (m.)

דורון

[Doron] = gift

דוש

[Dush] = to tread on; trample

דחל

[Dəhel] = [verb] to fear, be afraid (a) + (מן) of

דחלתא

[Dihəltha] = fear [f.]

דיד-

[Did-] = of; belonging to

דייתא

[Dayyathá] = eagle

דילמא

[Dilmá] = perhaps

דִּין

[Din] = [verb] to judge

דִּינָא

[Dina] = judgment

דַּיָּינָא

[Dayyáná] = judge

דִּיקְלָא

[Diqlá] = palm tree

דְּכָא

[Dəkha] = [verb] to be pure; (pa.) to purify

דְּכַר

[Dəkhar] = to remember

דִּכְרָא

[Dikhrá] = a male

דִּל-

[Dil-] = in order that

דְּלָא

[Dəlá] = that…not; lest

דלק

[Dəlaq] = to burn

דמא

[Dəmá] = [verb] to be like; (pa.) to liken

דמותא

[Dəmuthá] = image; likeness

דמיך

[Dəmeykh] = to sleep

דמכותא

[Damkhuthá] = sleep; death

דמע

[Dəma'] = to weep

דמעתא

[Dem°ətha] = tear (of the eye) [f.]

דעתא

[Da'thá] = knowledge; opinion; view

דקיק

[Dəqiq] = small; young (adj.)

דרכא

[Darkhá] = way; manner (m.)

דרש

[Dərash] = to expound; interpret

ה

הָא

[Há] = behold!

הֲדַסָא

[Hadasá] = myrtle (f.)

הֲוָא

[Həwa] = [verb] to be, become

הֵימִין

[Heymeyn] = to believe

הֵיכְלָא

[Heykhálá] = temple, palace

הָכָא

[Hakha] = here

הָכֵין

[Hakheyn] = thus, so

הַלֵּיךְ

[Halleyk] = [verb] to walk (pa.)

הֲלָן

[Halán] = there

הֲנָא

[Haná] = to be pleasant; to please

הֲנָייתָא

[Hanaythá] = enjoyment; benefit

הֲפָךְ

[Həfakh] = to turn 'the back' or 'the face'

הֲרֲהֵר

[Harher] = to meditate, criticize

הֲרֵי

[Harey] = Lo! Behold!

ו

-ו

[Wa-] = and

*always connects to another word

ויי

[Way] = Alas!

ולד

[Wəlad] = offspring; child (m.)

ז

זבִין

[Zaveyn] = to sell (pa.)

זבַן

[Zəvan] = [verb] to buy (e); (pa.) to sell

זהִיר

[Zəhir] = [verb] to guard, beware (pe.)

זוּגָא

[Zugá] = a couple; pair

זוִויי

[Zawey] = instead of (prep.)

זוִיתָא

[Zawithá] = corner

זוּן

[Zun] = to nourish; support

זוע

[Zu'] = [verb] to be moved, stirred (intrans.)

זימנא

[Zimná] = time

זיעתא

[Zi'athá] = sweat

זיקא

[Ziqá] = a shooting star; comet

זיתא

[Zaytá] = olive

זכא

[Zəkhá] = to be pure

זכותא

[Zəkhuthá] = righteousness, innocence

זליל

[Zalil] = cheap (adj.)

זמין

[Zameyn] = to invite (pa.)

זמנא

[Zimná] = time

זנא

[Zəná] = to play the harlot

זניתא

[Zanyáthá] = harlot

זער

[Zə'ar] = to be small

זעיר

[Za'eyr] = small (adj.)

זפתא

[Zifthá] = pitch (f.)

זרע

[Zəra'] = to sow; plant

זרעא

[Zar'á] = seed

זרעיתא

[Zar'ithá] = family (f.)

זרק

[Zəraq] = to cast; throw

ח

חביב

[Habib] = beloved

חבט

[HabaT] = to beat

חבל

[Havel] = to ruin, destroy (pa.)

חבר

[Haver] = to bind (pa.)

חברא

[Havrá] = companion (m.)

חברתא

[Həvarthá] = companion (f.)

חבש

[Havash] = to imprison

חגא

[Hagá] = festival

חדא

[Hədá] = [verb] to rejoice

חדת

[Hadat] = new [adj.] חדתא [f.] (Hadthá)

חדת

[Haddeth] = to make new (pa.)

חוב

[Hub] = [verb] to owe; be wrong; (pa.) to convict

חובא

[Hobá] = debt

חוט

[HuT] = to sew

חוס

[Hus] = [verb] to spare; pity

חור

[Hawar] = to be white

חורנא | חוריתא

[Horáná / Horaythá] = another; next (m. / f.)

חושבנא

[Hushbáná] = calculation (m.)

חזא

[Həza] = [verb] to see; (ethp.) to appear

חזיר

[Hazir] = pig

חזיר

[Hazeyr] = swineherd

חזק

[Hazaq] = to tie up

חזר

[Hazar] = to go around, return, turn back

חטא

[HaTá] = to sin

חטף

[HaTaf] = to snatch away

חיא

[Həyá] = [verb] to live; (aph.) to save

חייא

[Hayyá] = life

חייב

[Hayyav] = indebted, owing (adj.)

חיור

[Hiwar] = white (adj.)

חיויא

[Hiwyá] = serpent (m.)

חיטא

[HiTá] = wheat

חיילא

[Haylá] = strength, force

חכינא

[Hakiná] = large snake

חכים

[Hakim] = wise [adj.]

חכם

[Hakham] = to know, recognize

חוכמתא

[Hukhməthá] = wisdom [f.]

חלב

[Halav] = to milk

חלבא

[Halvá] = milk

חלם

[Halam] = to dream

חלמא

[Helmá] = dream (m.)

חלף

[Halaf] = [verb] to change, pass by

חלף

[Həláf] = for, instead of

חלץ

[Halatz] = to undress, to untie the shoe

חלקא

[Helqá] = field

חמא

[Hamá] = to see (pe.)

חמי

[Hammey] = to show (pa.)

חמד

[Hamad] = to covet; desire

חמים

[Hamim] = hot (adj.)

חמע

[Hama'] = to be sour, leavened (pe.); to ferment (aph.)

חמרא

[Hamrá] = wine [m.]

חמרא

[Hamárá] = (male) donkey

חנותא

[Hanuthá] = a shop (f.)

חנם

[Hinam] = gratis (adv.)

חנק

[Hanaq] = to choke; strangle

חסדא

[Hisdá] = love; charity (f.)

חסיד

[Hasid] = meek; pious (adj.)

חסל

[Hasal] = to cease, finish

חסר

[Hasar] = to lack

חפא

[Hafá] = to cover

חצא

[Hatzá] = to pick one's teeth

חקלא

[Haqlá] = field [m.]

חרשא

[Háráshá] = sorcerer

חרשיתא

[Harshithá] = sorceress

חשא

[Hashá] = to whisper

חשב

[Hashav] = to think, reckon (u)

חשד

[Hashad] = to suspect

חשש

[Hashash] = to suffer

חתם

[Hatam] = to close up; seal

ט

טאב

[T'ev] = [verb] to be good; (aph.) to do good

טב

[Tav] = good [adj.]; very, very much [adv.]

טבאות

[Tava'uth] = well (adv.)

טבחא

[TavaHá] = butcher (m.)

טביתא

[Təbithá] = gazelle (f.)

טבל

[Təval] = to bathe

טהר

[Təhar] = to be clean

טובא

[Tuvá] = goodness, mercy

טוס

[Tus] = to fly

טוף

[Tuf] = to float

טורא

[Torá] = mountain (m.)

טחן

[TəHan] = to grind [corn]

טחנא

[TaHaná] = a mill

טייל

[Tayyel] = to walk (pa.)

טלטל

[TalTel] = to carry away, remove, lift

טליא

[Talyá] = boy

טליתא

[Talithá] = girl

טלק

[Təlaq] = to throw down

טמא

[Təma] = to be or become unclean

טמר

[Təmar] = to hide; conceal

טעא

[Tə'á] = to wander; go astray; forget

טעותא

[Ta'uthá] = idol (f.)

טעם

[Tə'am] = to taste (a)

טעונא

[Tə'oná] = a load

טפא

[Təfá] = to go out; to die out

טפח

[TəfaH] = to close

טפיח

[TaffeyH] = to clap one's hands (pa.)

טפל

[Təfal] = to besmear

טפלא

[Tiflá] = fingernail

טרח

[TəraH] = to toil

י

יא-

[Ye-] = Let...be + *enclitic pronoun*

יאי

[Ya'ey] = beautiful (m.) [adj.]

יאיא

[Yáyá] = beautiful (f.) [adj.]

יאות

[Ya'uth] = well, worthily (adv.)

יבל

[Yəval] = (aph.) אוביל [Oveyl] = to lead, conduct

יבש

[Yəvesh] = to be dry; wither

ידא

[Yədá] = hand (f.)

ידי

[Yəda] = (aph.) **אודי** [Odi] = to confess, thank

ידע

[Yədaᵓ] = [verb] to know; (aph.) to inform, make known

יהב

[Yəhav] = [verb] to give

יהודי

[Yəhuday] = Jew

יומא

[Yoma] = day; *constr. & abs.* (**יום**)

יומיא

[Yomáyá] = days [pl.]

יום דין

[Yom deyn] = today

יונתא

[Yonthá] = dove (f.)

יְזַף

[Yəzaf] = to borrow; (aph.) אוֹזֵיף **X** [Ozeyf] to lend

יְכַל

[Yəkhal] = to be able to

יָלֵד | יְלִיד

[Yəled | Yəlid] = [verb] to give birth to (a); (ethp.) to be born; (aph.) to beget

יְלַף

[Yəlef] = [verb] to learn (a)

יַמָּא

[Yamá] = the sea

יְמָא

[Yəma] = to swear

יְנַק

[Yənaq] = [verb] to suck (pe.); (aph.) to suckle אוֹנֵיק **X** [Oneyq]

יַעֲלָא

[Ya'alá] = wild goat

317

יְקַר

[Yəqer] = to roast

יְקַר

[Yəqar] = [verb] to be heavy (a); (aph.) to honour

יַקִּיר

[Yaqir] = precious; dear (adj.)

יְרִי

[Yərey] = to permeate

יְרוּשְׁלֶם

[Yərushlem] = Jerusalem

יַרְחָא

[YirHá] = month

יְרִידָא

[Yəridá] = market-place

יַרְקָא

[Yarqá] = vegetables

יְרַת

[Yəret] = [verb] to inherit (a)

ירתותא

[Yirthuthá] = inheritance, legacy

ישׁו

[Yeshu] = Jesus

ישׁוע

[Yeshu'] = Jesus

יתב

[Yǝtav] = [verb] to sit down, sit; dwell

יתמא

[Yatmá] = orphan [m.]

יתר

[Yǝtar] = [verb] to gain, abound, remain over

יתיר

[Yathir] = more (+ מן) than

כך

‑כ

[K-] = like; as; according to

כא

[Ka'] = here

כאן

[Ka'n / Ka'an] = here

כבר

[Kəvar] = long ago; now; already

כבש

[Kəvash] = to tread, press, crush

כד

[Khad] = when; while

כדון

[Kadun] = now (adv.)

כדן

[Kədan] = to put to work

כדין

[Kədeyn] = thus; at this time

כהא

[Kəhá] = to be dim

כהנא

[Kahaná] = priest

כובא

[Kubá] = thorn (m.)

כודנא

[Kudná] = a mule

כוותא

[Kawthá] = a window (f.)

כות-

[Kəwat-] = like

כוזתא

[Kuzthá] = wine pitcher; jug

כוכבא

[Kukhbá] = star (m.)

כּוֹל

[Kol] = all, every

כּוּתִי

[Kutay] = a Cuthite; Samaritan

כּוֹתֶל

[Kotal] = a wall

כִּיסָא

[Kisá] = a purse

כִּיסָא

[Keysá] = thorn (m.)

כִּיפָא

[Keyfá] = a stone (m.)

כֵּיצַד

[Keytzad] = how? in what manner?

כִּיתְפָּא

[Kitpá] = shoulder (m.)

כָּךְ

[Kakh] = thus

כֹּל

[Kol] = all

כֹּל מָן דְּ-

[Kol man də-] = whoever

כַּלְתָא

[Kalthá] = a bride (f.)

כַּלְבָּא

[Kalbá] = a dog (m.)

כְּלוּם

[Kəlum] = anything; something

כְּלַל

[Kəlal] = to combine; generalize

כְּלִיל

[Kəlil] = crown, garland

כְּלָלָא

[Kəlálá] = a general rule

כְּמָא | כְּמַה?

[Kəmá | Kəmah?] = how many? how much?

כמרא

[Kumrá] = a heathen priest

כן

[Ken] = thus, so (adv.)

כנישתא

[Kənishthá] = synagogue (f.)

כנע

[Kəna'] = to oppress, humiliate; (ithpe.) to humble oneself, to bow

כסא

[Kasá] = cup (m.)

כסא

[Kəsa] = [verb] (pe. or pa.) to hide, cover

כספא

[Kispá] = silver (m.)

כעס

[Kə'as] = to be angry

כְּפַל

[Kəfal] = to double

כְּפַר

[Kəfar] = to deny + (-בְּ)

כְּפְרָא

[Kafrá] = village (m.)

כְּרוּב

[Kəruv] = cabbage (m.)

כְּרְמָא

[Karmá] = a vineyard (m.)

כְּרְסָא

[Kəreysá] = womb, bowels

כּוּרְסִיא

[Kursyá] = throne, divan

כְּרְעָא

[Kar'á] = leg (f.)

כְּשַׁר

[Kəshar] = to be right, fit, proper

כתב

[Kətav] = [verb] to write (o)

כתבא

[Kətává] = book, scripture; writing; document

כתבתא

[Kətavthá] = handwriting; writing

כתפא

[Katpá] = shoulder (m.)

ל

-ל

[Lə-] = to, for [prep.]

לֹא

[Lá] = not, no (*negative particle*)

לִבָא

[Livá] = heart

לְבֵשׁ

[Ləbesh] = [verb] to put on; to clothe oneself (a)

לְבוּשָׁא

[Ləbushá] = garment, clothing

לְהַט

[LəhaT] = to burn; be passionate

לָהֵן

[Lahen] = therefore; whither

לוחא

[LuHá] = table (m.)

לוט

[LuT] = [verb] to curse

לוי

[Ləwey] = to join; to accompany (pe.) (pa.)

לחהא

[LaHmá] = bread

לחש

[LəHash] = to whisper

לחישתא

[LəHishthá] = a whisper; a spell (f.)

לית (לא + אית)

[Layt (Lá + It)] = there is not, there are not

ליכא

[Likhá] = there is not; none

ליליא

[Leylyá] = night [f.]

לִימֵן

[Limeyn] = harbour

לִיסְטָא

[LisTá] = a robber

לִיקוּח

[Liqu'aH] = purchase (m.)

לִישָׁנָא

[Lisháná] = tongue; language

לְכַלֵךְ

[Lakhlekh] = to soak

לְמָה

[Ləmah] = why?

לְעָא

[Lə'á] = to toil, work, study

לְעֵיל

[Lə'eyl] = above; over; upwards

לְקָא

[Ləqá] = to be beaten; (aph.) to beat, thrash

לִקַח

[LəqaH] = to buy

לִקַט

[LəqaT] = to pick up; gather

לִרַע

[Ləra'] = to the ground; below

מם

מ- = מן

[M- = Min] = from + noun, adverb

מא

[Má] = what?

מאה

[Məʼah] = one hundred

מאי

[Mai] = what?

מאן

[Man] = who?

מבוע

[Məbuʼ] = a well, spring (m.)

מבלעדי

[Mibalʼadey] = without (prep.)

מגורא

[Məgurá] = neighbor (m.)

מגירא

[Məgirá] = neighbor (m.)

מגירתא

[Məgirthá] = neighbor (f.)

מגוסא

[Məgusá] = a dish, dinner (m.)

מגלא

[Maglá] = sickle (m.)

-מד

[Mid-] = because; since [prefix]

מדאתא

[Mada'thá] = tribute, tax, fine

מדינתא

[Mədinthá] = province, town

מה

[Mah] = what?

-מה ד

[Mah də-] = whatever

מהו

[Mahu] = what is it? how is it?

מהולא

[Məhulá] = a sieve (m.)

מהן

[Mahan] = who?

מהל

[Məhal] = to circumcise

מובלא

[Muvlá] = a load; burden (m.)

מוך

[Mukh] = to sink (*Hollow root verb*)

מוכס

[Mokhes] = a tax collector (m.)

מולתא

[Multhá] = a mule (f.)

מועדא

[Mo'adá] = a festival (m.)

מוקדשא

[Muqdəshá] = a sanctuary (m.)

מות

[Mut] = to die; (*perfect*) מית

מותא

[Mothá] = death [m.]

מותנא

[Motaná] = pestilence (m.)

מזון

[Mazon] = food (m.)

מזיק

[Maziq] = a demon

מחי

[MaHHey] = to forbid

מחק

[MəHaq] = to scrape off

מחרא

[MaHrá] = tomorrow

מטא

[MəTá] = to reach, arrive, to happen to (pe.); (aph.) אמטי
[AmTey] = to bring, fetch

מטקסא

[MəTaqsá] = silk

מטרא

[MiTrá] = rain (m.)

מי

[Mi] = while, when (adv.)

מיד

[Miyad] = at once (adv.)

מיהו

[Mihu] = however, but

מייא

[Mayyá] = water (m.)

מיכל

[Meykhal] = food (m.)

מִיכָן

[Mikhen] = from now

מִילוּל

[Milul] = word; speech (m.)

מִילְתָא

[Meylthá] = word (f.)

מִינָא

[Miná] = kind, class (m.)

מִית

[Mit] = dead (adj.)

מִיתוּתָא

[Mithuthá] = death (f.)

מְכִיוָן

[Mikheywan] = likewise; accordingly

מוּכְסָא

[Mukhsá] = tax collector (m.)

מְלָא

[Məlá] = to be full (pe.)

מְלִי

[Malley] = to fill, complete (pa.)

מְלְאֲכָא

[Mal'akhá] = angel (m.)

מַלְבְּנִיקָיָא

[Malbniqáyá] = pomegranates (m.pl.)

מִלְחָא

[MilHá] = salt (m.)

מַלָחָא

[MaláHá] = a sailor (m.)

מַלְיָיא

[Malyá] = abundance (m.)

מְלַךְ

[Məlakh] = [verb] to reign; to consult

מַלְכָּא

[Malká] = king

מַלְכוּתָא

[Malkutá] = kingdom [f.]

מלכתא

[Malkthá] = queen (f.)

מליל (מלל)

[Mallel] = to speak, talk (pa.)

ממונא

[Mammoná] = money, wealth, riches (m.)

מן

[Min] = from (prep.)

מנא

[Məná] = to reckon, calculate (pe.)

מני

[Mani] = to elect; appoint (pa.)

מנין

[Minyán] = number (m.)

מנע

[Məná'] = to withhold, refuse

מנתא

[Mənathá] = a share; allotment

מסאב

[Məsa'av] = unclean (adj.)

מסאנא

[Məsa'ná] = shoe (m.)

מסור

[Masor] = traitor, informer (m.)

מסכין

[Miskheyn] = poor (adj.)

מסנתא

[Məsanthá] = basket (f.)

מסר

[Məsar] = to hand over; surrender

מסורתא

[Masorthá] = tradition (f.)

מסתא

[Misthá] = enough, sufficiency (f.)

מעיא

[Mə'áyá] = bowels, belly (m.pl.)

מעלא

[Ma'alá] = entrance (m.)

מערתא

[Mə'arthá] = cave (f.)

מפלתא

[Mapalthá] = fall; ruin (f.)

מפני

[Mifney] = because of (prep.)

מפתחא

[MiftəHá] = a key (m.)

מצודתא

[Mətzudá] = a net (m.)

מצותא

[Mitzwəthá] = a command; a charity

מרא

[Márá] = Lord, Master (m.)

מרא

[Mərá] = to be bitter (pe.); (pa.) to embitter, make sad

340

מרגליתא

[Margálithá] = pearl (f.)

מרחמן

[MəraHmán] = merciful (adj.)

מרתא

[Marthá] = mistress (f.)

משחא

[MishHá] = oil (m.)

משח

[MəshaH] = to anoint; besmear

משיחא

[MəshiHá] = messiah

משיחתא

[MəshiHathá] = a rope (f.)

משקיא

[Mashqyá] = a drink [*fluids*]

מתיבא

[Mətivá] = a seat, abode (m.)

מתן

[Mətán] = to delay (pe.); (aph.) to wait

מתנתא

[Matanthá] = gift (f.)

מתקל

[Matqal] = weight, responsibility (m.)

נן

נבח

[NəbaH] = to bark

נגב

[Nəgev] = to be dry; become dry

נגד

[Nəgad] = [verb] to draw (e)

נגס

[Nəgas] = to eat; dine

נגע

[Nəga'] = to touch (pe.); (pa.) to smite

נדבא

[Nidbá] = a free gift (m.)

נדר

[Nədar] = to vow

נדרא

[Nidrá] = a vow (m.)

נהג

[Nəhag] = to guide, lead

נהק

[Nəhaq] = to cry; to bray

נהר

[Nəhar] = to shine, to be bright

נהורא

[Nəhurá] = light (m.)

נהרא

[Nahará] = river (m.)

נוכרי

[Nukhray] = a heathen (m.)

נום

[Num] = to sleep; slumber (*Hollow root verb*)

נוקבתא

[Nuqvəthá] = a female (f.)

נוקניקא

[Nuqaniqá] = sausage

נורא

[Nurá] = fire, flame (m.)

נזיר

[Nazir] = Nazirite

נזף

[Nəzaf] = to rebuke

נזק

[Nəzaq] = to suffer injury

נחש

[NaHHesh] = to practice sorcery

נחשא

[NəHáshá] = copper (m.)

נחתם

[NaHthom] = a baker (m.)

נחתומר

[NaHthomar] = a bakery (m.)

נטורא

[Nátorá] = watchman, guardian

נטלא

[NaTlá] = a ladle

נטר

[NəTar] = to watch, guard

ניה

[Ni'aH] = right, good (adj.)

נימוסא

[Nimosá] = law (m.)

נכס

[NəHas] = to slaughter

נכר

[NKR] = (aph.) אכיר [Akhir] = to know, recognize

נסא

[Nisá] = miracle (m.)

נסב

[Nəsav] = to lift up, take away (a)

נסיון

[Nisayon] = a test, a miracle (m.)

נְסַךְ

[Nəsakh] = [verb] to pour (o)

נְסַע

[Nəsa'] = to move (pe.); (aph.) אָסַע [Asa'] = to remove

נְסַק

[Nəsaq] = to go up (pe.); (aph.) to bring up

נְעַל

[Nə'al] = to tie a shoe

נְעָמִיתָא

[Na'amithá] = an ostrich (f.)

נְפַח

[NəfaH] = to blow up; whistle

נְפַל

[Nəpal] = [verb] to fall (e)

נְפַק

[Nəfaq] = [verb] to go out (o); (aph.) to expel

נְפַשׁ

[Nəfash] = to become much or many

נפשא

[Nafshá] = soul; self [f.]

נפשתא

[Nafshátá] = souls; selves [pl.]

נפתי

[Nafthi] = Nabatean

נצ(י)א

[Nitztzá] = blossom (m.)

נצח

[NətzaH] = to succeed, conquer

נקא

[Nəqa'] = to be clean (pe.); (pa.) to cleanse

נקז

[Nəqaz] = to cut

נקי

[Naqi] = clean (adj.)

נקף

[Nəqaf] = to strike (pe.); (aph.) to knock

נְקַר

[Nəqar] = to pierce

נְקַשׁ

[Nəqash] = to strike, smite

נְשָׁא

[Nəshá'] = to forget (pe.); (ithpe.) אִינְשִׁי [Inshi] to be forgotten

נְשָׁא

[Náshá] = man (m.)

נְשַׁיָּיא

[Nəshayá] = women [pl. of 'אִתָּא' (Ithá) 'woman']

נְשִׁיָּיא

[Nəshiyá] = prince (m.)

נְשַׁם

[NSHM] = (ithpa.) אִינְשַׁם [Inasham] = to recover; get well

נְשִׁיק

[Nəsheq] = [verb] (pe.) (o) (a) to kiss; (pa.) to kiss

נתן

[Netan] = [verb] to give (*only imperfect & infinitive are used*) (e)

נתר

[Nətar] = [verb] to wither and fall (a)

ס

סאב

[Sa'ev] = [verb] to defile (pa.); (pe.) to be unclean

סב

[Sáv] = old

סבותא

[Sávuthá] = old age (f.)

סבורא

[Sávurá] = a reasoner (m.)

סבל

[Səval] = to carry a load

סבר

[Səbar] = [verb] (pe.) (a) to think, suppose, hope

סגד

[Səgad] = [verb] to worship, bow down (o)

סגולא

[Səgolá] = a cluster of grapes (m.)

351

סְגִי

[Səgey] = to grow in size or number

סַגְרִיר

[Sagrir] = a storm, hurricane (m.)

סְדִינָא

[Sədiná] = a linen sheet (m.)

סְדַר

[Sədar] = to arrange, put in order

סְהֵד

[Səhed] = [verb] (pe.) (a) to be a witness

סָהֲדָא

[Sahadá] = martyr, witness [m.]

סָהֶדְתָא

[Sáhedthá] = martyr, witness [f.]

סוּלָם

[Sulám] = ladder (m.)

סום

[Sum] = [verb] to tie, adjust (*Hollow root verb*); (pa.) to mark, define

סוס

[Sus] = a horse (m.)

סחא

[SəHá] = to bathe, wash oneself

סיב

[Siv] = old, grey (adj.)

סיפרא

[Sifrá] = book (m.)

סכא

[Səkhá] = to look

סכין

[Sakin] = knife (m.)

סכל

[Səkhal] = to see clearly (pe.); (ithpa.) אסתקל [Istaqal] to look at

סכם

[Səkham] = to count, reckon (pe.); (aph.) to agree

סכן

[Səkhen] = to be in danger; to be dangerous (pe.); (pa.) to endanger

סכנתא

[Sakanthá] = danger (f.)

סלק

[Səleq] = [verb] to go up (pe.); (pa.) to remove

סמא

[Səmá] = to be blind

סמא

[Samá] = poison, powder (m.)

סמך

[Səmakh] = to lay the hand upon, to ordain, to support

סמק

[Səmeq] = to be red

סנא

[Səná] = [verb] to hate

סנדל

[Sandal] = a sandal (m.)

סערתא

[Sə'arthá] = barley (f.)

ספק

[Səfaq] = [verb] to be enough (a)

ספר

[SFR] = (pa.) ספיר [saffer] = to shave; (ithpa.) איספר [Isafer] to be shaved

ספרא

[Sifrá] = book (m.)

ספרא

[Sáfrá] = a scribe (m.)

ספרותא

[Safruthá] = office of the scribe (f.)

סקא

[Saqá] = sackcloth (m.)

סרא

[Sərá] = to stink

סרה

[SəraH] = to be corrupt, to sin

סתוא

[Sitwá] = winter (m.)

סתם

[Sətam] = to shut up, seal

ע

עבד

['Abad] = [verb] to do, make (e); (shaph.) to subjugate

עבדא

['Abdá] = servant, slave

עבורא

['Aburá] = grain, crops (m.)

עבידתא

['Abidthá] = work, employment (f.)

עבר

['Abar] = [verb] to cross, pass by, transgress (a)

עבירתא

['Abeyrthá] = sin [f.]

עגול

['Igul] = a circle, a cake (m.)

עגל

['Agal] = to be round (pe.); (pa.) to roll

עגלתא

['Agalthá] = a basin (f.)

עד

['Ad] = until, as far as

עד ד-

['Ad də-] = while; until

עד דלא

['Ad dəlá] = before

עדיין

['Adayin] = still, yet

עדר

['Adar] = to help

עובדא

['Ubdá] = a fact; anecdote (m.)

עוד

['Ud] = still, yet

עוד ד-

['Ud də-] = too, besides

עוֹל

['Ol] = yoke (m.)

עוּל = עלל

['Ul = 'Alal] = to come in; enter

עוֹלָא

['Awlá] = perversity, disease, evil

עוֹלָם

['Ulem] = powerful [in magic]; young (adj.)

עוּן

['Un] = (pa.) עַיֵּין ['Ayyen] to guard, watch

עוּק

['Uq] = to be sorrowful, in distress

עוּר

['Ur] = to arouse, awaken, awake

עוֹרָא

['Orá] = skin (m.)

עוֹרְבָא

['Orbá] = crow, raven (m.)

עזא

['Izá] = goat (m.)

עטש

['ATash] = to sneeze

עיזקא

['Izqá] = a fetter, a ring (m.)

עילא

['Eylá] = height, heaven (m.)

עילתא

['Ilthá] = a falsehood (f.)

עיינא

['Ayná] = eye [f.]

עיסקא

['Isqá] = business (m.)

עיסתא

['Isthá] = dough (f.)

עיצתא

['Eytzthá] = counsel (f.)

עכברא

['Akhbárá] = mouse

על

['Al] = upon, concerning, unto

עלא

['Alá] = a leaf (m.)

עליב

['Aliv] = wretched; poor (adj.)

עלל

['Alal] = to enter; go in (pe.); (aph.) אעיל [A'ell] to bring in

עללא

['Alalá] = produce (m.)

עלמא

['Almá] = world, age - (לעלם) [lə'alam] forever

עלעל

['Al'ol] = a hurricane (m.)

עִם

['Im] = with (prep.)

עַמָּא

['Amá] = people, nation

עַמּוּדָא

['Ammudá] = a pillar (m.)

עַמְרָא

['Amrá] = wool (m.)

עֲנָא

['Aná] = [verb] to answer

עִנְווָן

['Eynwán] = humble, meek (adj.)

עַנְוְותָא

['Anwáthá] = a chance (f.)

עֻנְקָא

['Inqá] = neck, throat

עֲסוּקָא

['Isuqá] = management, concern (m.)

עֵסַק

['Asaq] = to busy oneself (pe.); (ithpa.) to study

עֵסְקָא

['Isqá] = business, habit, character (m.)

עַפְרָא

['Aprá] = dust (m.)

עֲצַל

['Atzal] = to be slothful (pe.)

עֲצַר

['Atzar] = to keep back, restrain

עֲקַר

['Aqar] = to uproot (pe.); (ithpe.) to be uprooted, ruined

עֲרוּבְתָא

['Aruvthá] = sunset (f.)

עַרְבִי

['Arbay] = Arab (m.)

עַרְבֵב

['Arbev] = to disturb

עָרֵל

['Arel] = uncircumcised (adj.)

עַרְסָא

['Arsá] = a bed (m.)

עֲרַק

['Araq] = to flee (o)

עֲשִׁיק

['Ashiq] = expensive, very rare (adj.)

עֲשַׂר

['Asser] = to tithe (pa.)

עֲתַד

['Atted] = to prepare (pa.)

עֲתִיד

['Atid] = ready, destined, certain

עֲתִיק

['Athiq] = old (adj.)

עֲתִיר

['Athir] = rich (adj.)

פף

פגל

[Paggel] = to render unfit as sacrifice

פגול

[Pigul] = something rejectable (m.)

פגע

[Pəga'] = to meet (pe.); (ithpe.) to happen

פה

[Poh] = here (adv.)

פוגלא

[Puglá] = a radish (m.)

פוח

[Pu'aH] = to breath, expire

פומא

[Pumá] = mouth (m.)

פונדקין

[Pundqin] = inn, hotel (m.)

פונדקאי

[Pundqay] = an innkeeper (m.)

פורא

[Porá] = fruit (m.)

פורנא

[Purná] = dowry (m.)

פחא

[PaHá] = contempt (m.)

פחת

[PǝHath] = to become less; lose money; collapse

פחתא

[PaHathá] = decrease, loss, a pit

פטל

[PǝTal] = a piece, a bite, a bit (m.)

פטים

[PaTim] = fat (adj.)

פטר

[PǝTar] = to set free, release (pe.); (pa.) to divorce

פיוסא

[Piyusá] = conciliation, an apology (m.)

פילא

[Pilá] = ivory (m.)

פילי

[Piley] = a town gate (f.)

פייס

[Payyes] = to persuade, appease (pa.)

פייסונא

[Paysoná] = a mason (m.)

פייסנתא

[Paysanthá] = a mason's guild (f.)

פינך

[Pinakh] = a dish

פינקסא

[Pinaqsá] = a tablet, a book (m.)

פיסחא

[PisHá] = Passover (m.)

פִּיסְתָּא

[Pisthá] = a piece of bread (f.)

פִּיתָא

[Pitá] = a piece (of bread) (m.)

פִּיתְרָא

[Pitrá] = a wine vessel (m.)

פְּלָא

[Pəlá] = to cut open

פְּלַג

[Pəlag] = to divide; to share

פַּלְגָּא

[Palgá] = a portion; a half

פְּלַח

[PəlaH] = to work, to worship

פְּלַט

[PəlaT] = to emit, to escape

פְּלַל

[Pəlal] = to argue, to debate

פִּלְפֵּל

[Pilpál] = pepper, grain (m.)

פָּנָא

[Pəná] = to turn, turn away, depart

פַּנְיָא

[Panyá] = evening (m.)

פַּסָא

[Pasá] = a stripe, a portion (m.)

פְּסִיקָא

[Pəsiqá] = a collection (of money)

פְּסַע

[Pəsa'] = to walk, waddle

פְּסַק

[Pəsaq] = to cut off, break loose

פָּעֵל

[Po'al] = a workman (m.)

פְּצַל

[Pətzal] = to divide, peel, skim

369

פָּקַד

[Fəqad] = to command, store up

פִּקְדּוֹנָא

[Piqdoná] = deposit (m.)

פָּקַח

[PəqaH] = to open the eyes

פָּרָא

[Pərá] = to run

פַּרְגִּיתָא

[Pargithá] = chicken (f.)

פַּרְדֵּס

[Pardes] = paradise, park (m.)

פָּרוּשׁ

[Parush] = a Pharisee

פָּרַח

[PəraH] = to fly

פְּרִיטָא

[PəriTá] = small change, coin (m.)

פרנס

[Parnes] = to provide for, manage

פרנס

[Parnás] = manager, steward (m.)

פרנסא

[Parnásá] = nourishment (m.)

פרס

[Pəras] = to split, spread

פרסי

[Parsay] = a Persian (m.)

פרסם

[Parsem] = to publish; to defame, denounce

פרע

[Pəra'] = to expose, to take vengeance

פרק

[Pəraq] = to redeem

פרוקנא

[Pəruqná] = redemption (m.)

פרש

[Pərash] = to separate, depart

פשפש

[Pashpesh] = to search, grope

פשר

[Pəshar] = to distinguish, explain

פתא

[Pitá] = a piece of bread, a loaf

פתח

[PətaH] = to open

פתחא

[PitHá] = door, an opening

פתור

[Pator] = table (m.)

פתרא

[Pitrá] = interpretation (m.)

פיתרא

[Pitrá] = a large wine jar (m.)

צץ

צאא

[Tzə'á] = to defile, dirty, soil

צבחד | צבחר

[TzivHad | TzivHar] = a little, few (m.)

צבע

[Tzəba'] = to dip, dye

צבעא

[Tzabá'á] = a dyer (m.)

צדיק

[Tzadiq] = righteous (adj.)

צדוקי

[Tzəduqay] = Sadducee (m.)

צואה

[Tzo'áh] = excrement (f.)

צוד

[Tzud] = to hunt, to catch

צוֹם

[Tzum] = to fast

צוֹמָא

[Tzomá] = fasting, a fast (m.)

צוֹנַם

[Tzonam] = rock, granite (m.)

צוּר

[Tzur] = to tie, wrap up

צוֹרכָּא

[Tzurkhá] = need, necessity (m.)

צחָא

[TzəHá] = to thirst

צִיבּוּר

[Tzibur] = congregation (m.)

צַיָיד

[Tzayyad] = fisherman, hunter (m.)

צַיָיר

[Tzayyar] = a painter, embroiderer (m.)

צינתא

[Tzinthá] = cold (f.)

ציפדונא

[Tzifdoná] = scurvy (m.)

צלא

[Tzəlá] = to bend, to bow (pe.); (pa.) to pray

צלא

[Tzəlá] = to cook, to roast

צלב

[Tzəlav] = to hang, to crucify

צלותא

[Tzəlothá] = prayer (f.)

צלותא

[Tzəlawáthá] = prayers [f.pl.]

צלוחיתא

[TzəluHithá] = bottle, flask (f.)

צלי

[Tzalley] = to pray (pa.)

צְלַל

[Tzəlal] = to ring; to be clear; to cast a shadow

צַלְמָא

[Tzalmá] = an image (m.)

צַלְצֵל

[Tzaltzel] = to shout

צְמָא

[Tzəmá] = to trim (nails)

צְמַד

[Tzəmad] = to bind, attach

צְמַח

[TzəmaH] = to sprout

צְמַק

[Tzəmaq] = to shrivel, dry

צְמַת

[Tzəmath] = to gather together, assemble

צְנַן

[Tzənan] = to be cold

צְנַע

[Tzəna'] = to guard

צְעַר

[Tzə'ar] = to despise, disgrace, shame (pe.); (pa.) to afflict, grieve, annoy

צַעְרָא

[Tza'ará] = disease, pain (m.)

צְפָא

[Tzəfá] = to look at, watch, observe

צַפְצֵף

[Tzaftzef] = to whistle, chirp

צְפַר

[Tzəfar] = to whistle

צַפְרָא

[Tzafrá] = early morning (m.)

צִפְרָא

[Tziprá] = a bird (m.)

צְרוֹר

[Tzəror] = a pebble (m.)

צָרִיךְ

[Tzərikh] = to need

צָרִיךְ

[Tzərikh] = it is necessary; 'must' (auxiliary)

צְרַךְ

[Tzərakh] = to need

צְרַר

[Tzərar] = to wrap, tie up

ק

קבורתא

[Qəvurthá] = burial (f.)

קבל

[Qəbal] = to cry out, complain against (pe.)

קבל

[Qabbel] = [verb] (pa.) to receive, accept; (aph.) to confront

קבלא

[Qabálá] = tradition, post-mosaic scripture (f.)

קבל | קובלא

[Qəbel | Quvlá] = before, in the presence of

קבע

[Qəba'] = to fix, to fasten

קבעא

[Qib'á] = appointment (f.)

קבר

[Qəbar] = [verb] to bury (o)

קָדוֹשׁ

[Qadosh] = holy (adj.)

קְדָלָא

[Qədálá] = the neck (m.)

קַדֵּם

[Qaddem] = to go or get before; to go to meet; to do beforehand

קֳדָם

[Qadam] = before [prep.]

קַדְמָי

[Qadmay] = first, former (m.)

קְדַשׁ

[Qədash] = to be sacred (pe.)

קַדֵּשׁ

[Qaddesh] = [verb] (pa.) to sanctify

קְהָלָא

[Qahalá] = congregation (m.)

קוּלָא

[Qolá] = a bowl, jar (m.)

קוּם

[Qum] = to rise, stand up; (pa.) to establish

קוּמֵי

[Qomey] = before (prep.)

קוּמֵי ד-

[Qomey də-] = before that…

קוּפָא

[Qufá] = basket (m.)

קוּפְדָא

[Qufdá] = meat (m.)

קוּפְתָא

[Qufthá] = basket, tub, sack (f.)

קוּרְקַס

[Qurqas] = a clasp; ring; key (m.)

קוּשְׁיָא

[Qushyá] = difficulty (m.)

קֹזֶן

[Qazzen] = to calculate

קְטָא

[QəTá] = to bite off; gain (in a lottery)

קְטִין

[QaTin] = thin, emaciated (adj.)

קְטַל

[QəTal] = to kill

קִטְמָא

[QiTmá] = ashes, powder (m.)

קְטַע

[QəTa'] = to hew down

קְטַר

[QəTar] = to bind, tie up

קִידְרָא

[Qidrá] = a pot (m.)

קִיטְרָא

[Qitrá] = a knot (m.)

קייטא

[QayTá] = summer (m.)

קיטון

[Qiton] = a room, chamber (m.)

קייט

[QayyaT] = fig-drier (m.)

קיים

[Qəyám] = a covenant (m.)

קיים

[Qayyem] = to keep alive

קילוסא

[Qilusá] = praise (m.)

קים

[Qim] = to live, continue

קיסא

[Qeysá] = wood, chips (m.)

קלא

[Qálá] = voice (m.)

קָלוֹן

[Qalon] = a disgrace, idol (m.)

קְלָא

[Qəlá] = to be disgraced

קָלִיל

[Qalil] = cheap, light (adj.)

קְלֵיס

[Qaleys] = to praise; celebrate, dance

קְלַק

[Qəlaq] = to throw, cast

קִלְקֵל

[Qalqel] = to ruin, corrupt; damage

קִמְחָא

[QamHá] = flour (m.)

קַמְצָא

[Qamtzá] = locust (m.)

קִנָּא

[Qiná] = a nest, swarm (m.)

קְנָא

[Qəná] = to acquire, take possession

קַנְדִילָא

[Qandilá] = a candle, lamp (m.)

קַנְטֵר

[QanTer] = to rebuke

קַנְקַנָא

[Qanqaná] = plough (m.)

קְסַס

[Qəsas] = to turn sour

קְפַד

[Qəfad] = to be sensitive, irritable; (ithpe.) אִיקְפַד [Iqfad] = to be angry

קְפַח

[QəfaH] = to strike, to wound; to rob

קְצָא

[Qətzá] = to break (bread)

קְצִיעֲתָא

[Qətzi'thá] = a fig-harvest (f.)

קְצַץ

[Qətzatz] = to cut; to make a covenant

קְרָא

[Qərá] = to call, read, to recite

קְרֵב

[Qərev] = to be near, to draw near (pe.); (pa.) to bring near

קְרִיב

[Qareyv] = near (adj.)

קְרָבָא

[Qərává] = war (m.)

קְרְבְנָא

[Qarbáná] = sacrifice (m.)

קְרוּנְתָא

[Qaronthá] = a wagon, a cart (f.)

קְרְטַס

[QarTes] = a paper, document (m.)

קְרִייָה

[Qiryah] = a small town (f.)

קְרִייָא

[Qaryá] = a Bible verse

קְרִיצְתָא

[Qəritzthá] = day-break (f.)

קְרְנָא

[Qarná] = a horn (m.)

קְרְקַע

[Qarqa'] = soil (m.)

קְרַץ

[Qəratz] = to rise early

קְרְתָא

[Qarthá] = a town (f.)

קְשָׁא

[Qəshá] = to be hard, difficult (pe.); (pa.) to perplex

קְשִׁי

[Qashey] = hard (adj.)

קְשִׁיא

[Qashyá] = a difficulty, strong objection (f.)

קְשִׁיוּתָא

[Qashyuthá] = hardness, obstinacy (f.)

ר

ראש

[Resh] = head

ראשית

[Reshith] = beginning (f.)

רב

[Rab] = chief, master (m.)

רב

[Rab] = great (adj.)

רבא

[Rabá] = great [adj.] *emphatic of* רב

רבב

[Rəvav] = to be a teacher

רבוא

[Ribo] = ten thousand, a myriad (m.)

רבותא

[Rəvuthá] = dignity, glory (f.)

רבא

[Rəvá] = to be or become great; to come of age

רביא

[Ravyá] = a boy (m.)

רביעתא

[Rəvi'athá] = rain (f.)

רביתא

[Rabithá] = interest (f.)

רבון

[Ribon] = lord, master (m.)

רבע

[Rəva'] = to lie down, recline

רברבא

[Ravrəvá] = a great man (m.)

רגג

[Rəgag] = to desire

רגז

[Rəgaz] = to tremble

רגיל

[Ragil] = accustomed to (m.) *used like a participle*

רגלא

[Riglá] = a foot (m.)

רגש

[Rəgash] = to tremble (pe.); (aph.) to observe

רדא

[Rədá] = to chastise

רהט

[RəHaT] = to run

רוא

[Rəwá] = to be drunk

רובא

[Rubá] = majority (m.)

רוחא

[RuHá] = spirit; wind (f.)

רום | רים

[Rum | Rim] = to be high; lift; remove (pe.); (aph.) to remove

רומי

[Romi] = Rome

רומי

[Romay] = Roman (adj.)

רומנתא

[Rumánthá] = pomegranate (f.)

רומשא

[Romshá] = evening (m.)

רוק

[Ruq] = to spit out

רחיא

[RiHyá] = millstone (m.)

רחם

[RəHem] = to love (pe.) & (pa.)

רחמא

[RaHmá] = friend (m.)

רחמן

[RaHamán] = merciful (adj.)

רחמתא

[RaHəmthá] = friend (f.)

רחץ

[RəHatz] = to lean on; trust

רחק

[RəHeq] = to be distant; alienated

רחוקא

[RiHuqá] = separation, distance (m.)

רחיק

[RaHiq] = distant, far off (adj.)

ריבוא

[Rivo'] = a myriad (m.)

ריבתא

[Rivthá] = maiden (f.)

ריוא

[Reywá] = sight, appearance (m.)

ריח

[Rey'aH] = to breath (pe.); (aph.) אריח (Arey'aH) to smell

ריחיא

[ReyHayá] = millstones (m.pl.)

ריקן

[Reyqan] = empty (adj.)

רירא

[Rirá] = spittle (m.)

ריש

[Reysh] = head, top (m.)

רכב

[Rəkhav] = to ride

רכיך

[Rakikh] = soft, tender (adj.)

רְכַן

[Rəkhan] = to lean (pe.); (aph.) to bend

רמא

[Rəmá] = to throw

רמיותא

[Rəmyuthá] = deceit (f.)

רמשא

[Ramshá] = evening (m.)

רעא

[Rə'á] = to feed, tend; to delight in

רעם

[Rə'em] = to be high (pe.); (aph.) to raise

רעע

[Rə'a'] = to break in pieces

רפא

[Rəfá] = to be loose, free (pe.); (aph.) to let loose, leave alone

רצון

[Ratzon] = favor, good will, desire (m.)

רק

[Raq] = only, except

רקד

[Rəqad] = to dance (pe.) & (pa.)

רקיע

[Rəqi'a] = firmament (m.)

רקע

[Rəqa'] = to stretch, spread

רקק

[Rəqaq] = to spit

רשותא

[Rəshuthá] = authority, permission (f.)

רשיא

[Rashyá] = a creditor (m.)

רשל

[Rəshal] = to be weak, flaccid

רשיעא

[Rashi'á] = wicked (adj.)

רתח

[RəthaH] = to boil, to be hot

רתק

[Rəthaq] = to knock

שׁ

שָׁאַל

[Shə'al] = to ask a question, ask a favor

שְׁאִילְתָּא

[Shə'eylthá] = a request (f.)

שְׁבָא

[Shəvá] = to take captive

שָׁבוּיָא

[Shavoyá] = Sabaean; captor, raider

שְׁבַח

[ShəvaH] = to rise (pe.); (pa.) to praise

שְׁבָחָא

[ShəvaHá] = praise, song (m.)

שְׁבַע

[SHB'] = (ithpa.) אִשְׁתָּבַע (Ishtaba') to swear

שְׁבַע

[Səba'] = to be satisfied

שְׁבַק

[Shəbaq] = to leave, to forsake, to allow

שְׁבַר

[Shəvar] = to break

שִׁבְשָׁא

[Shivshá] = a branch, bush (m.)

שְׁבִשְׁתָּא

[Shəvishthá] = twig, branch (f.)

שְׁבַת

[Shəvat] = to observe the Sabbath

שַׁבְתָּא

[Shabthá] = Sabbath (m.)

שְׁגַח

[ShəgaH] = to look (pe.); (aph.) to care for

שְׁגַר

[Shəgar] = to put forth, shed (tears)

שְׁדוֹךְ

[Shədokh] = to be quiet, peaceful

שְׁהֵד

[Səhed] = to be a witness

שַׁהֲדוּתָא

[Sahaduthá] = testimony (f.)

שׁוּבְתָא

[Shubthá] = Sabbath (f.)

שְׁוָא

[Shəwá] = to be alike

שְׁוִי

[Shəwey] = to be alike

שַׁוְיָא

[Shawyá] = a bed, a couch for eating (m.)

שׁוֹעִיתָא

[Shaw'ithá] = tale, talk (f.)

שׁוּק

[Shuq] = market, street (m.)

שׁוּר

[Shur] = a city wall (m.)

שׁוּרְבָּא

[Shurbá] = heat (m.)

שְׁזַג

[Shəzag] = to wash, rinse

שְׁזַרְתָּא

[Shezarthá] = cord, spine, skeleton (f.)

שְׁחִיָא

[ShiHyá] = bend, armpit (m.)

שְׁחַק

[ShəHaq] = to rub, grind

שַׁחֲרִיתָא

[ShaHarithá] = morning (f.)

שְׁטַף

[ShəTaf] = to overflow; wash away

שִׁיחָא

[ShiHá] = a pit, ditch (m.)

שיירתא

[Shəyyarthá] = a caravan (f.)

שימשא

[Shimshá] = the sun (m.)

שין

[Sheyn] = tooth

שינתא

[Sheynthá] = sleep (f.)

שיצי

[Shetztzi] = to be ended, perish (pa.)

שייר

[Shayyer] = to leave behind, reserve (pa.)

שירא

[Sheyrá] = neck-chain (m.)

שכונתא

[Shəkhunthá] = neighborhood (f.)

שכח

[ShəkhaH] = to forget (pe.); (aph.) to find, to be able

שלוחא

[ShəluHá] = messenger (m.)

שלח

[ShəlaH] = to send

שלט

[ShəlaT] = to rule, authorize

שליחותא

[ShəliHuthá] = errand, commission (f.)

שלם

[Shəlem] = to be finished (pe.); (aph.) to finish; (pa.) to recompense, pay

שלמא

[Shəlámá] = peace, health, welfare (m.)

שמא

[Shəmá] = name (m.)

שמאלא

[Shəmá'lá] = the left hand (m.)

שְׁמוּעֲתָא

[Shəmu'athá] = report, tradition, decision, law (f.)

שְׁמַט

[ShəmaT] = to loosen, slip off, be released

שְׁמִיטְתָא

[ShəmiTthá] = release; cancellation of debts (f.)

שְׁמַיָּא

[Shəmayá] = Heaven (m.)

שְׁמַע

[Shəma'] = to hear (pe.); (aph.) to proclaim

שַׁמֵּשׁ

[Shammesh] = to minister (pa.)

שִׁמְשָׁא

[Shimshá] = the sun (m.)

שְׂנָא

[Səná] = to hate (pe.)

שׁנא

[Shəná] = to repeat, to change, to be different (pe.); (pa.) to change

שׁני

[Səney] = to hate (pe.)

שׁנץ

[Shənatz] = to squeeze

שׁנתא

[Shanthá] = a year (f.)

שׁעא

[Shə'á] = to cover over, smooth (pe.); (ithpa.) אשׁתעי (Ishta'i) = to converse pleasantly; tell a story

שׁער

[Sha''er] = to calculate (pa.)

שׁערא

[Sa'ará] = hair (m.)

שׁעריא

[Sa'aryá] = barley (m.pl.)

שעתא

[Sha'thá] = hour (f.)

שפך

[Shəfakh] = to pour out

שפר

[Shəfar] = to be beautiful, acceptable

שק

[Saq] = a sack (m.)

שקל

[Shəqal] = to receive, take

שקלא

[Shiqlá] = a shekel (m.)

שקע

[Shəqa'] = to sink

שקקא

[Shəqáqá] = street (m.)

שקרא

[Shiqrá] = a falsehood (m.)

שָׁקָר

[Shaqár] = liar (m.)

שָׂרָא

[Sárá] = a prince (m.)

שֵׁר

[Sher] = a chain, ring (m.)

שְׁרָא

[Shərá] = to loosen

שַׁתָּא

[Shathá] = a year (m.)

שְׁתָא

[Shəthá] = to drink

שְׁתַק

[Shətaq] = to be silent, shut up (o)

ת

תאב

[Thə'ev] = to desire, want

תאנתא

[Tə'eynthá] = fig (f.)

תבלא

[Thavlá] = spice (m.)

תבנא

[Thivná] = straw (m.)

תבע

[Thəva'] = to seek, to ask

תבר

[Thəvar] = to break (pe.); (pa.) to smash

תבשיל

[Thavshil] = broth (m.)

תגר

[Thagár] = a merchant (m.)

תדיר

[Thədir] = constant (adj.)

תואר

[Tho'ar] = look, appearance (m.)

תוב

[Thuv / Tuv] = to go back, return

תומא

[Thumá] = garlic (m.)

תורא

[Thorá] = an ox (m.)

תורתא

[Thorthá] = a heifer, a calf (f.)

תורעתא

[Tur'athá] = a gate (f.)

תות

[Thot] = under (prep.)

תּוּתִי

[Thotey] = under (prep.)

תְּחוּמָא

[ThəHomá] = limit, boundary (m.)

תְּחוּת

[ThəHot] = under, behind, instead of (prep.)

תְּחַל

[THḤL] = (aph.) אַתְחֵל (AthHel) = to begin

תֵּיבוּתָא

[Theyvuthá] = a chest, an ark (f.)

תֵּייטְרוֹן

[Thəyyatron] = theatre (m.)

תִּינוֹק

[Thinoq] = a child, a boy (m.)

תְּכַף

[Təkhaf] = to join closely, to connect

תַּכְרִיכָא

[Thakhrikhá] = shroud (m.)

תְלָא

[Thəlá] = to hang, suspend, to depend on

תַּלְגָּא

[Thalgá] = snow (m.)

תַּלְמוּדָא

[Talmudá] = Talmud, teaching, study

תַּלְמִידָא

[Talmidá] = a disciple, student (m.)

תְלַשׁ

[Thəlash] = to pluck off

תַּמָּן

[Thamán] = there (adv.)

תַּמְרָא

[Thámrá] = date [fruit]; palm tree (m.)

תְּנָא

[Tǝná] = to repeat, study, teach (pe.); (pa.) to teach

תַּנָּאי

[Thanay] = a teacher (m.)

תנורא

[Thənurá] = an oven (m.)

תסברא

[Thisbárá] = treasure, treasury (m.)

תעלא

[Tha'alá] = a jackal (m.)

תעניתא

[Tha'anithá] = fasting (f.)

תיפייא

[Thifyá] = a pot, a stove (f.) *emphatic state*

תפש

[Thəfas] = to seize, to bind with a spell

תקל

[Thəqal] = to weigh

תקן

[Thaqqen] = (pa.) to reform, repair; (aph.) to prepare, ordain

תקנתא

[Thaqanthá] = remedy, reform (f.)

תרגומא

[Targumá] = translation (m.)

תרגם

[Targem] = to read, translate

תרנגולא

[Tharngolá] = a cock, a hen (m.)

תרס

[Thəras] = to challenge, to oppose

תרעא

[Tar'á] = door, gate (m.)

תרתר

[Tharther] = to scatter dust or loose earth

תשועתא

[Thəshu'thá] = salvation (f.)

תשש

[Thəshash] = to be weak, sick

תשיש

[Tashish] = sick, weak (adj.)

Part III

I)   Basic Aramaic Phrases

The following section will contain reconstructed phrases of the Jewish Palestinian Aramaic Language. All of the phrases will be transliterated into Latin letters so that the reader will be able to easily pronounce the phrases and at the same time learn how to read Aramaic without the diacritic marks.

*Remember that Jewish Palestinian Aramaic did not originally use diacritic marks as it was a system that was created later on.

The phrases will follow this format throughout this section:

Ex.

אלהא טב

[Elaha Tav] = God is good

a. Greetings & Farewells

שלמא!

[Shlama!] = Hello!

שלם לך!

[Shlam lakh!] = Hello! [to a man]

שלם ליך!

[Shlam likh!] = Hello! [to a woman]

שלם לכון!

[Shlam lakhun!] = Hello! [to several people]

שלמא עליכון!

[Shlama ᵓalaykhun!] = Peace be upon you! [Greeting]

בריך צפרא!

[Brikh Tzafrá!] = Good morning!

בריך רמשא!

[Brikh Ramshá!] = Good evening!

ליליא טב!

[Leylya Tav!] = Good Night!

זיל בשלמא!

[Zel bashlama!] = Go in peace! Goodbye!

זיל עם אלהא!

[Zel 'im Elaha!] = Go with God! Goodbye!

b. Basic Conversational Phrases

אִין

[In] = Yes

לֹא

[La] = No

מַה שְׁלָמַךְ?

[Mah shlamakh?] = How are you? [to a man]

מַה שְׁלָמִיךְ?

[Mah shlamikh?] = How are you? [to a woman]

אֲנָא טַב וֵאַנְתְּ?

[Ana Tav wa-ant?] = I am well, and you?

אנא טב

[Ana Tav] = I am well

אלהא מברך יתך!

[Elaha məbarrek yatakh!] = God bless you! [to a man]

אלהא מברך יתיך!

[Elaha məbarrek yatikh!] = God bless you! [to a woman]

מה שמך?

[Mah shmakh?] = What is your name? [to a man]

מה שמיך?

[Mah shmikh?] = What is your name? [to a woman]

שמא דידי...

[Shma didi...] = My name is...

מן היכא אנת?

[Min heykha ant?] = Where are you from?

מנן אנת?

[Minan ant?] = Where are you from?

מנא אנת?

[Mina ant?] = Where are you from?

מנן את?

[Minan at?] = Where are you from?

אנא מן ירושלם

[Ana min yərushlem] = I am from Jerusalem

מה בעית?

[Mah ba'eyth?] = What do you want? [to a man]

מַה בְּעֵית?

[Mah ba'yáth?] = What do you want? [to a woman]

מַא רְגַגְת?

[Ma rag-gath?] = What do you desire? [to a man]

מַא רְגַגְת?

[Ma rag-gáth?] = What do you desire? [to a woman]

מַאי תָּאבַת?

[Mai tha'vath?] = What do you want? [to a man]

מַאי תָּאבַת?

[Mai tha'váth?] = What do you want? [to a woman]

מַאי תַּבְעַת?

[Mai thab'ath?] = What do you seek? [to a man]

421

מאי תבעת?

[Mai thab'áth?] = What do you seek? [to a woman]

לאן אזלת?

[Lə'an azlath?] = Where are you going? [to a man]

לאן אזלת?

[Lə'an azlath?] = Where are you going? [to a woman]

מה עבדת?

[Mah 'abdath?] = What are you doing? [to a man]

מה עבדת?

[Mah 'abdath?] = What are you doing? [to a woman]

אית לי למאזל

[It li ləmezal] = I have to go

אית לי למאזל השתא

[It li ləmezal hashthá] = I have to go now

אית לי למאזל האדנא

[It li ləmezal ha'idáná] = I have to go now

אית לי למיעבדיה

[It li ləmey'bdeyh] = I have to do it

אתינא בשלמא

[Athey-na bashlámá] = I come in peace [when a man is speaker]

אתינא בשלמא

[Athya-na bashlámá] = I come in peace [when woman is speaker]

אתית?

[Atheyth?] = Are you coming? [to a man]

אתית?

[Athyath?] = Are you coming? [to a woman]

משכחנא למעדר לך

[MashkaH-na ləme'dar lakh] = I can help you

משכחת למעדר לי?

[MashkHath ləme'dar li?] = Can you help me?

מהימין באלהא

[Məheymeyn b-Eláhá] = I believe in God

לית כלום הכא

[Leyt klum hakha] = There isn't anything here

לית לי כלום

[Leyt li klum] = I don't have anything

אלהא חזא כל חטאיא

[Eláhá haze kol HəTa'yá] = God sees all sins

אלהא טב

[Eláhá Táv] = God is good

למה שבקתני!

[Ləmah shəbaqthani!] = Why have you left me? Why have you forsaken me?

למה שנית יתי?

[Ləmah saneyth yati?] = Why do you hate me? [to a man]

למה שנית יתי?

[Ləmah sanyath yati?] = Why do you hate me? [to a woman]

אנא נשית כתבי

[Ana nəshith kətavi] = I have forgotten my book

אנא שכחית ספרי

[Ana shəkhHeyth sifri] = I have forgotten my book

למה בזית יתי?

[Ləmah bazeyth yati?] = Why do you despise me? [to a man]

למה בזית יתי?

[Ləmah bazyath yati?] = Why do you despise me? [to a woman]

רחימנא יתיך

[RaHeym-na yatikh] = I love you [man to a woman]

רחמנא יתך

[RaHma-na yatakh] = I love you [woman to a man]

אמירנא לך קושטא

[Ameyr-na lakh qoshTá] = I tell you the truth

חזינא כל מא דעבדת

[Haze-na kol ma də-'abdath] = I see everything that you do

יומא דין שבתא

[Yomá deyn shavthá] = Today is the Sabbath

את שפירא

[At shafirá] = You are beautiful [to a woman]

מאן את?

[Man at?] = Who are you?

שמיענא כל מה דאתון אמרין

[Shame'-na kol mah də-Atun ámrin] = I hear everything that you all say

בעינא דאת תעדר לי

[Ba'ey-na də-at te'edar li] = I want that you help me

אנא יכיל עדיר לך

[Ana yakheyl 'ader lakh] = I can help you

מה בעית?

[Mah ba'eyth?] = What do you seek?

בעינא קושטא

[Ba'ey-na qoshTá] = I seek the truth

רגיגנא למאזל לירושלם

[Rageyg-na ləmezal li-rushlem] = I want to go to Jerusalem

אתרא דין מיתליט

[Atrá deyn mithliT] = This place is cursed

אנא אמליל עמך

[Ana emallel 'imakh] = I will speak with you

אנא אמליל עמיה

[Ana emallel 'imeyh] = I will speak with him

ממלילנא ארמיא

[Məmallel-na Aramáyá] = I speak Aramaic

אנא אתרגים כתבא דין

[Ana atargem kətavá deyn] = I will translate this book

מייתינא לך מייא

[Mayte-na lakh mayya] = I am bringing you water

מתרגימנא כתבא דין

[Mətargem-na kətavá deyn] = I am translating this book

כלהון ייתדינון

[Koləhun yithdinun] = All of them will be judged

אלהא ייתי דיניה על ארעא

[Eláhá yaythey dineyh ʻal arʼa] = God will bring his judgment upon the earth

צריכנא למיכול

[Tzareykh-na ləmeykhul] = I need to eat

צריכנא למאזל

[Tzareykh-na ləmezal] = I need to go

אין בעית, תקביל

[In baʼeyth, təqabbel] = If you ask, then you shall receive

היכא ביתא דידך?

[Heykha baytá didakh?] = Where is your home?

לא ידיענא

[La yadeʼ-na] = I don't know

לא רגיגנא למידע

[La rageyg-na ləmeyda'] = I don't want to know

אנא לא אישכח

[Ana la eyshkaH] = I will not forget

אנא לא אישא

[Ana la eyshe] = I will not forget

ידעת?

[Yad'ath?] = Do you know?

מתבוננא

[Mithbonen-na] = I understand

לא מתבוננא

[La mithbonen-na] = I do not understand

מתבננת יתי?

[Mithbonnath yati?] = Do you understand me?

אנא איהב לך מתנתא

[Ana ihav lakh mathanthá] = I will give you a gift

רגיגנא למאלף ארמיא

[Rageyg-na ləmelaf aramáyá] = I want to learn the Aramaic

יהבית כתבא לאחוך

[Yehveyth kətavá l-aHukh] = I gave the book to your brother

יהבתה לי לחמא

[Yəhavthah li laHmá] = You gave me bread

גוברא גנב כתבי

[Guvná gənav kətavi] = The man stole my book

גנבתה כתבי?

[Gənavthah kətavi?] = Did you steal my book?

נאכול בשרא וגובנא עם חמרא

[Nekhul bisrá wəguvná 'im Hamrá] = We shall eat meat and cheese with wine

דקיסר הבון לקיסר ודאלהא הבון לאלהא

[Dəqeysar həvun ləqeysar wadeláhá həvun leláhá] = "Give to Caesar what is Caesar's and give to God what is God's"

c. Common Commands

תא!

[Thá!] = Come! [to a man]

תיי!

[Tháy!] = Come! [to a woman]

תון!

[Thun!] = Come! [to several people]

תא עמי!

[Thá 'imi!] = Come with me!

תא להכא!

[Thá ləhakha!] = Come here!

זיל!

[Zel!] = Go! [to a man]

זלין!

[Zlin!] = Go! [to a woman]

זלון!

[Zlun!] = Go! [to several people]

זיל לתמֹן!

[Zel ləthamán!] = Go there!

תון נאזל!

[Thun nezel!] = Let's go!

שבוק לי!

[Shbuq li!] = Forgive me!

שבוק לן!

[Shbuq lan!] = Forgive us!

הב לי מייא!

[Hav li mayya!] = Give me water!

הב לי...!

[Hav li...!] = Give me...!

הב לן...!

[Hav lan...!] = Give us...!

אכול!

[Akhul!] = Eat!

תון נאכול!

[Thun nekhul!] = Let's eat!

פתח תרעא!

[FtaH tar'a!] = Open the door!

עול!

['Ull!] = Enter!

מליל!

[Mallel!] = Speak! [to a man]

מללין!

[Malləlin!] = Speak! [to a woman]

מללון!

[Malləlun!] = Speak! [to several people]

אמר לי...!

[Iṃar li...!] = Tell me!

תון נמליל!

[Thun nəmallel!] = Let's talk!

אמר לי קושטא!

[Imar li qoshTá!] = Tell me the truth!

לא תאזל!

[La tezel!] = Don't go!

לא תעבדיה!

[La te'ebdeyh!] = Don't do it!

לא תמריה!

[La timreyh!] = Don't say it!

לא תאתא!

[La tithe'!] = Don't come!

לֹא תֵעוּל!

[La te'ull!] = Don't enter!

לֹא תִקְטְלַן!

[La teqTlan!] = Don't kill me!

נַשִׁיק יָתִי!

[Nashsheq yati!] = Kiss me! [woman to a man]

נַשִׁקִין יָתִי!

[Nashshqin yati!] = Kiss me! [man to a woman]

תִיב!

[Teyv!] = Sit! Sit down!

תִיב עִמָּנַן!

[Teyv 'imanan!] = Sit with us!

תון ניתיב תמן!

[Thun netheyv thamán!] = Let's sit there!

תון ניתיב הכא!

[Thun netheyv hakha!] = Let's sit here!

רחט!

[RəHaT!] = Run!

שקול!

[Shqul!] = Take this!

תון נהדר למדינתא!

[Thun nehdar ləmdinthá!] = Let's return to the city!

תון נתוב למדינתא!

[Thun nathuv ləmdinthá!] = Let's return to the city!

תון נהדר לכּפרא!

[Thun nehdar ləkafrá!] = Let's return to the city!

תון נתוב לכּפרא!

[Thun nathuv ləkafrá!] = Let's return to the city!

לא תרחט!

[La tirHeT!] = Don't run!

לא תפרא!

[La tipre!] = Don't run!

שתוק!

[Shtuq!] = Be quiet! Shut up! [to a man]

שותקין!

[Shutqin!] = Be quiet! Shut up! [to a woman]

שׁותקון!

[Shutqun!] = Be quiet! Shut up! [to several people]

עדר לי!

['Ədar li!] = Help me!

אשכח כתבי!

[AshkaH kətavi!] = Find my book!

אשכחיה!

[AshkHeyh!] = Find it!

הליך עמי!

[Halleykh 'imi!] = Walk with me!

תון נהליך לתמן!

[Thun nəhalleykh ləthamán!] = Let's walk there!

תון נעבדיה!

[Thun ne'edbeyh!] = Let's do it!

תון נאזל השתא!

[Thun nezel hashthá!] Let's go now!

אייתי לי---!

[Aythe li…!] = Bring me…!

אייתי לי כתבא!

[Aythe li kətavá!] = Bring me the book!

בעי ותישכח!

[Ba'ey wətashkaH!] = Seek and ye shall find!

שאל ותקבל!

[Shə-al wət-qabbel!] = Ask and ye shall receive!

בעי יתי ותשכחן!

[Ba'ey yati wətashkHan] = Seek me, and ye shall find me!

למד לי!

[Ləmad li!] = Teach me!

אליף לי!

[Allef li!] = Teach me!

II)   Numbers 1-10

Masc.   Fem.

Masc.	Fem.		
חד	חדא	Had [m] / Hada [f]	1
תרין	תרתין	Threyn [m] / Thartheyn [f]	2
תלתא	תלת	Thlatha [m] / Thlath [f]	3
ארבעא	ארבע	Arbaᵓa [m] / Arbaᵓ [f]	4
חמשא	חמש	Hamsha [m] / Hamesh [f.]	5
שיתא	שית	Sheytha [m] / Sheyth [f]	6
שבעא	שבע	Shəbaᵓa [m] / Shəbaᵓ [f]	7
תמניא	תמני	Thamanya [m] / Thamaney [f]	8
תשעא	תשע	Təshaᵓa [m] / Təshaᵓ [f]	9
עסרא	עסר	ᵓAsara [m] / ᵓAsar [f]	10

*Remember that Numbers have to match the gender of the Nouns that they modify.

*Numbers 2-10 go with plural Nouns

*Number one is only used with singular Nouns

Sources Used:

תלמוד ירושלמי *(Talmud Yerushalmi) - The Extended Version.* 22 volume set. (n.d.). עוז והדר (Oz Vehadar). 15 Harmich Rd. South Plainfield, NJ 07080. Print.

MGRNB: אדוני

Other Publications and Books by Author:

[B'ajlom ii Nkotz'i'j Publications and KDP Publishing]

"B'ajlom ii Nkotz'i'j Publications' Tz'utujiil Maya Phrasebook: Ideal for Traveling in Sololá, Guatemala C.A., 3rd Edition" (2019)

"B'ajlom ii Nkotz'i'j Publications' Ch'ol Maya Phrasebook: Ideal for Traveling in Tumbalá, Chiapas, México, 2nd Edition" (2018)

"B'ajlom ii Nkotz'i'j Publications' Yucatec Maya (Maayat'aan) Phrasebook: Ideal for Traveling in Península de Yucatán, México, 2nd Edition" (2018)

"B'ajlom ii Nkotz'i'j Publications' Kazakh Phrasebook: Ideal for Traveling throughout Kazakhstan, 1st Edition" (2020)

"B'ajlom ii Nkotz'i'j Publications' K'iche' Maya Phrasebook: Ideal for Traveling throughout Guatemala, Central America, 1st Edition" (2020)

"B'ajlom ii Nkotz'i'j Publications' Bosnian Phrasebook: Ideal for Traveling throughout Bosnia & Herzegovina, 1st Edition" (2020)

"B'ajlom ii Nkotz'i'j Publications' Haitian Creole Phrasebook: Ideal for Traveling throughout Haiti, 1st Edition" (2020)

"B'ajlom ii Nkotz'i'j Publications' Kyrgyz Phrasebook: Ideal for Traveling throughout Kyrgyzstan, 1st Edition" (2020)

"B'ajlom ii Nkotz'i'j Publications' Luxembourgish Phrasebook: Ideal for Traveling throughout Luxembourg, 1ˢᵗ Edition" (2020)

"B'ajlom ii Nkotz'i'j Publications' German Phrasebook: Ideal for Traveling throughout Germany, 1ˢᵗ Edition" (2020)

"B'ajlom ii Nkotz'i'j Publications' Russian Phrasebook: Ideal for Traveling throughout the Russian Federation, 1ˢᵗ Edition" (2020)

"B'ajlom ii Nkotz'i'j Publications' Kurdish Phrasebook: Ideal for Traveling in Kurdistan, 1ˢᵗ Edition" (2020)

"B'ajlom ii Nkotz'i'j Publications' Yezidi Phrasebook: Ideal for Traveling within Yezidi Communities around the World, 1ˢᵗ Edition" (2020)

"B'ajlom ii Nkotz'i'j Publications' Classical & Modern Nahuatl Phrasebook: Ideal for Traveling throughout Central México, 1ˢᵗ Edition" (2020)

"B'ajlom ii Nkotz'i'j Publications' Catalan Phrasebook: Ideal for Traveling throughout Northeastern Spain, 1ˢᵗ Edition" (2020)

"B'ajlom ii Nkotz'i'j Publications' Galician Phrasebook: Ideal for Traveling throughout Northwestern Spain, 1ˢᵗ Edition" (2020)

"B'ajlom ii Nkotz'i'j Publications' Quechua Phrasebook: Ideal for Traveling in the Andean Regions of South America, 1ˢᵗ Edition" (2020)

"B'ajlom ii Nkotz'i'j Publications' Guatemalan Spanish Phrasebook: Ideal for Traveling throughout Guatemala, 1ˢᵗ Edition" (2020)

"B'ajlom ii Nkotz'i'j Publications' Guide to Classical Syriac, 1ˢᵗ Edition" (2020)

"B'ajlom ii Nkotz'i'j Publications' Guide to Coptic, 1ˢᵗ Edition" (2020)

"B'ajlom ii Nkotz'i'j Publications' A Linguistic Guide to Hebrew, Aramaic, Syriac & Arabic, 1ˢᵗ Edition" (2021)

"B'ajlom ii Nkotz'i'j Publications' Guide to Jewish Babylonian Aramaic, 1ˢᵗ Edition" (2021)

All publications are available on Amazon.com and Booksamillion.com

B'ajlom ii Nkotz'i'j Publications ™

FOR ANY QUESTIONS FEEL FREE TO CONTACT US AT:

Biinpublications@gmail.com

Printed in Great Britain
by Amazon

22116366R00260